Positive Mindset Mastery
2 Books in 1

Develop a Positive Mindset and Attract the Life of Your Dreams

+

How to Stop Being Negative, Angry, and Mean

Richard Banks

Positive Mindset Mastery

Positive Mindset Mastery

© Copyright 2020 - All rights reserved.

The content contained within this book may not be reproduced, duplicated or transmitted without direct written permission from the author or the publisher.

Under no circumstances will any blame or legal responsibility be held against the publisher, or author, for any damages, reparation, or monetary loss due to the information contained within this book. Either directly or indirectly.

Legal Notice:

This book is copyright protected. This book is only for personal use. You cannot amend, distribute, sell, use, quote or paraphrase any part, or the content within this book, without the consent of the author or publisher.

Disclaimer Notice:

Please note the information contained within this document is for educational and entertainment purposes only. All effort has been executed to present accurate, up to date, and reliable, complete information. No warranties of any kind are declared or implied. Readers acknowledge that the author is not engaging in the rendering of legal, financial, medical or professional advice. The content within this book has been derived from various sources. Please consult a licensed professional before attempting any techniques outlined in this book.

By reading this document, the reader agrees that under no circumstances is the author responsible for any losses, direct or indirect, which are incurred as a result of the use of the information contained within this document, including, but not limited to, — errors, omissions, or inaccuracies.

Positive Mindset Mastery

Develop a Positive Mindset and Attract the Life of Your Dreams 11

Introduction 13

Chapter 1: Believing In Yourself 29

Self-knowledge 29

Accept that change happens 58

Summary 60

Chapter 2: The Power of Positive Thinking 63

The History 63

The Present 65

10 Ps for Reprogramming Your Mind 70

Positive energy 79

Summary 99

Chapter 3: Inferiority Complex and Self-Doubt 103

How Inferiority Complex Presents 105

History of the Inferiority Complex 108

Symptoms and Signs of Inferiority Complex 109

Risk Factors and Causes of Inferiority Complex 115

Dealing with an Inferiority Complex 119

Summary 125

Chapter 4: Managing Your Emotions 127

What Are Emotions? 127

Why Should You Manage Emotions? 134

Managing Emotions 139

How Does That Connect with a Positive Outlook? 145

Limiting beliefs 149

Summary 170

Chapter 5: Managing Your Relationships 173

Good Relationships? Why? 175

What Makes a Good Relationship? 177

Relationships at Work 179

Ten Tips to Keep Any Relationship Healthy 183

Difficult Relationships 187

Tips for Ending a Bad Relationship 189

Summary 195

Chapter 6: Neuro-Linguistic Programming 199

Dissociation 208

Content Reframing 213

Anchoring Yourself 218

Rapport 223

Persuasion and Influence 230

Summary 235

Chapter 7: Daily Rituals for a Positive Mindset 237

Why Rituals are Important 237

Morning Rituals 242

Before Bed Rituals 249

Summary 260

Chapter 8: Reaching Your Full Potential 263

7 Skills to Reach Your Full Potential 266

Dream, Believe, and Dare to Do 272

Summary 276

Conclusion 277

References 281

How to Stop Being Negative, Angry, and Mean 285

Introduction 287

Chapter 1: Thoughts Vs. Core Beliefs 293

Thoughts 294

Core Beliefs 295

Perception 300

Cognitive Distortions 305

Recap 312

Chapter 2: Emotions 313

What Can Influence Our Emotions? 315

The Things We Think Can Impact the Things We Feel 317

Can Emotions and Thoughts Be Changed? 318

Defense Mechanisms 319

How to Be the Boss of Your Emotions 327

Recap 345

Chapter 3: Shifting Your Mindset 347

Growth vs. Fixed Mindset 348

Handling Setbacks 351

Brain Plasticity 352

Main Differences Between Growth and Fixed Mindsets 362

Ways to Build Your Growth Mindset 364

Recap 373

Chapter 4: Understanding Negativity 375

What Counts as a Negative Thought? 376

Negativity Bias 377

What Causes Negative Thoughts? 381

Why Can't They Just Stop? 384

Types of Negativity 386

The Dangers of Negative Thoughts 389

Negativity in Relationships 392

Working Through Three Common Negative Thinking Patterns 396

Other Ways to Overcome Negativity 399

Recap 402

Chapter 5: Understanding Anger 405

How to Control Anger 406

When Does Anger Become a Disorder? 407

What Causes Anger 408

Everybody Has Triggers 415

Anticipating Your Anger 417

Tips to Help You Control Your Anger 418

Suppressing Your Emotions 425

Handling Strong Emotions 427

Recap 430

Chapter 6: Understanding Pessimism 433

Handling Pessimism 434

What Is Optimism? 437

Tips to Help You Think Positively 438

Recap 446

Chapter 7: Developing Awareness of Thoughts and Emotions 447

Emotional Self-Awareness 448

Developing Self-Awareness 449

Steps You Can Take to Develop Your Thoughts and Feelings 451

How to Develop Your Emotional Self-Awareness 453

Recap 460

Chapter 8: Reprogramming Your Mind 461

Reticular Activating System 463

Emotional Intelligence 465

Cognitive Behavioral Therapy 469

Mindfulness 469

Recap 486

Chapter 9: The Power of Gratitude 487

Gratitude Helps Your Relationships 488

Gratitude Gets Rid of Negativity 489

But How Can I Be Grateful? 490

Recap 492

Conclusion 495

References 499

Develop a Positive Mindset and Attract the Life of Your Dreams

---

Unleash Positive Thinking to Achieve Unbound Happiness, Health, and Success

Richard Banks

Positive Mindset Mastery

Introduction

"Be Positive"- So small a phrase, yet with such magnanimous impact on our lives. Sometimes we wonder, is it really that easy to be positive? Most days, we find ourselves struggling to deal with many problems, some within and some beyond our perception and control. An impending exam result, the responsibility of becoming a father, the untimely loss of a loved one, many problems could arise from the emotional fluctuations you go through in these situations. More often than not, it is highly possible that an individual could ignore the psychological and physical impacts of emotionally intensive scenarios in their life. This book is my attempt to help you identify problems that you may have been ignoring for quite some time. I have also invested my thoughts and opinions, combined with factual information, to showcase the importance of a positive mindset in solving various problems.

So, what are the problems we are talking about?

- Do you feel stuck in a job or relationship that you don't love anymore?
- Are you struggling to get a comfortable and relaxing night's sleep?

- Have you been feeling like you're missing out on all the fun and enjoyment in your life?
- Are you feeling overwhelmed and need help getting rid of negative thoughts?
- Are you struggling with low self-esteem or a lack of confidence to pursue your dreams?

If you have been experiencing any of these problems, then it is very likely that you are vulnerable to stress, anxiety, and a host of other psychological health issues such as low self-esteem, depression, and little motivation. As these issues develop gradually and manifest themselves in your mind and consciousness, you start feeling burdened by negative thoughts. The overwhelming feeling of negativity building up on your psyche could slowly impair your resolve in life.

Anxiety is a wicked friend. It takes without ever giving back. One thing happens, and before you know it, you are triggered to remember your childhood friend who one time stole your toy or your uncle when he promised a gift that you are still waiting for as an adult. The point is, you begin feeling anxious about one thing, and it gives birth to other things like anger and self-doubt in an unending spiral that only births more places to fall in the pits of despair.

Understandably, when you open a blog post, a newspaper article, or even see your friend's tweet-able advice to just 'think positively,' you might be suspicious and perhaps a little annoyed. You know that optimism is something to strive for, but you also know that it is not that easy.

There is good news.

You do not have to be unrealistic to change your point of view and become a more positive person.

You must admit to the darker aspects of a particular situation in the process of becoming more positive. Positive thinking is not about denial. It is about having hope and confidence in your ability to deal with the tough things that come at you. It is about remembering that no one thing is all negative every time. In the particularly darker storms of life, you can grab the sunnier takeaways and enjoy the moments of relief, regardless of their size.

If positivity does not naturally come to you, you are more familiar with anxiety than with enthusiasm for life, do not beat yourself up.

There are people born with a neural architecture (rose-colored glasses, if you may) that predisposes them to enjoy more positive emotions and to see only the best things in the world. Others come with grey-colored glasses, and that is their genetic lottery.

Before beginning to learn how to be a happier person, you do well to appreciate that wherever you fall, you matter, and the perspective you have to offer is critical, not just for yourself but for everyone around you. That said, it may be challenging for some people more than others to learn to be positive, but everyone can pick up the necessary skills.

Whether you want to leave the daily melancholy behind you and keep confident, or whether you simply want to conquer one area of your life that seems clouded by a shroud of negativity, this book is for you.

Here, you will learn past the commonly touted advice that, although well-intended, can feel empty - things like repeating a personal mantra at yourself or paying little attention to negative thoughts. You will understand the science behind the advice and be able to tailor it to yourself. You will reap the benefits of 'knowledge as power' because after reading through, you will know your 'why,' and as Nietzsche said, that will help you overcome any 'how.'

Say you want to pick a personal mantra. On the first day, you look yourself in the eyes and whisper how beautiful you are, but despite the passion you put to it, something still feels off. You realize that it is not easy to get comfortable with the practice, and any smidge of relief the exercise brings is taken away by the thought of how weird it is. What do you do then?

Or perhaps you want to pay less attention to the negative thoughts you have. You have realized that you get caught up in a loop of concern and worry. You overanalyze everything, and the rumination process causes your mood to plummet even further downward. You congratulate yourself, rightfully so, on the show of progress identifying what the problem is. You resolve to hold things lightly, but that resolve becomes fodder for further over-analysis. Before you know it, you are crippled, in a bad mood, and you do not even remember where it all started. What are you to do?

First, one mistake many people make is assuming that happiness just happens and that you can simply pursue it. However, happiness is a byproduct of being engaged in life. It is not like making money that you foster by analyzing your finances and coming up with an improvement plan. Thinking about making yourself happy will be the first sure sign that it backfires.

Secondly, negative thoughts are not strong enough to control you. You are strong enough to control them. Think of them like TV reruns that you have seen millions of times. Leave them playing in the background and focus on other things. It is a little like telling your mind 'hey, thank you for letting me know,' and then moving your attention elsewhere.

Optimism and a positive outlook are like muscles – the more you train them, the stronger they become.

Research shows that learning to see the half-full glass has many benefits. It can improve the quality of your life and could even extend your lifespan. Researchers at Harvard University studied 70,000 women for eight years. They found that the most optimistic of them had a 30% lower risk of dying from major death causes compared to the less optimistic women (American Journal of Epidemiology, 2016).

If you are not aware of it, positive thinking is not just about your outlook on life. It is also your attitude toward yourself, and that, as experts say, could affect your health. Some studies show that personality traits like pessimism and optimism could affect your wellbeing. Optimism is effective in stress management, which offers numerous benefits to health.

As earlier mentioned, positive thinking is not

the equivalent of burying your head in the proverbial sand and ignoring the unpleasant situations. It is about approaching the situations positively and productively – you expect the best to happen, not the worst. It is integrally tied to self-talk.

Self-talk is the constant stream of unspoken thoughts running in your head, which are either positive or negative. Some thoughts are informed by reason and logic, but others come from misconceptions you created because you lacked information. Research shows that if you continuously have negative thoughts, you may be a pessimist.

Research shows that positive thinking leads to:

- Lower depression rates
- Lower distress levels

- Better skills to cope with hardships and stress
- Better heart health
- Reduced risks of death from cardiovascular diseases
- Better physical and psychological wellbeing
- Greater resistance to the common cold

It is not yet clear why there are associations between positive thinking and these health benefits. One of the prevailing theories is that positive thinking will help you better cope with stress and thus reduce the harmful health effects of stress that your body experiences. Another school of thought holds that optimistic people live healthier lifestyles, have healthier diets, and get more physical activity.

Whatever the relation is, the benefits are

undeniable, and anyone can potentially enjoy them.

This book will teach you how to identify negative thinking so that you do not just focus on the negative aspects of a situation or blame yourself for bad things that happen.

You will learn how to turn negative thinking into positive thinking and the processes of investing practice and time into forming new habits. You will be able to identify the areas that need changing, live a healthy lifestyle, and talk to yourself in a way that will uplift you.

You cannot expect changes to happen overnight, but with practice, you can learn to criticize yourself less and accept yourself more. This will translate into you being more accepting of the world around you. When your mind is typically optimistic, you can handle whatever comes at you more constructively.

Lao Tzu is recorded as saying to 'watch your thoughts because they become words' (Lao Tzu, 1984). Your words become actions and, in turn, become a habit. Habits become character, and your character shapes your destiny. Otherwise stated, everyone has a set of messages playing over and over in their minds. The personal commentary will influence what you say, do, who you are, your relationships, and eventually your destiny.

There is never a better time to begin working on whatever is dysfunctional in your head than now. Your actions ripple and extend to all the corners of your life. You are part of a network, and how you live life affects the network and spreads to the whole world. A negative approach becomes a self-fulfilling prophecy. You begin to reap what you sow and attract what you are.

Concepts like the law of attraction, birds of a feather flocking together, and attracting what you think all testify to how positive thinking is crucial.

How then do you begin brightening your view of the world and infusing more positivity into the things you think? This book will answer this question and others on the topic. It will empower you to go forth and live a better life. If that sounds like what you care about, keep reading.

Positive Mindset Mastery

Chapter 1: Believing In Yourself

In this chapter, you will learn useful skills for staying positive. For example, how to have faith in your abilities, detoxing your mind, self-confidence, reaching your potential, shifting your mindset, and controlling your thoughts. All these, unless anchored on the correct knowledge, will not last and could quickly become more reasons to be anxious. They have to be based on self-knowledge.

Self-knowledge

The famous philosopher Socrates is believed to have said that the unexamined life is not worth living. When asked what all commandments in philosophy could be whittled down to, he said, 'know yourself.'

Knowing oneself is prestigious in today's culture and has been framed as the meaning of life. It can easily become cliché, so one wonders why self-knowledge is a good thing. What happens if you do not know yourself? How do you come to do it, and why is it so difficult to know oneself?

Self-knowledge refers to a specific kind of knowledge of a psychological or emotional nature. You can know the week that you were born or whether or not you are a morning person but still lack self-knowledge. Not everything you know about yourself is essential to know. Self-knowledge in this section is concerned with your inner psychological core –

what kind of person may you be attracted to and why? What are your talents? How are you when you receive feedback? What do you do when life frustrates you?

If you can answer these questions thoroughly, you can speak of yourself as someone who knows themselves well, and you can begin your journey to becoming a positive person.

Think of this process like digging for gold – you have to go deep to find the value. You cannot be afraid to find out what lies beneath the choices you make, the things that cause you to spiral, and your causes for anxiety.

Self-knowledge offers a route to fulfillment and a degree of happiness. If you do not know yourself, you are open to mistaking ambitions. The right knowledge of self gives you more chances for avoiding errors as you deal with others and as you make your life choices.

The main point of this section is to form a basis for reflection before you begin to adopt any of the things this book recommends. That way, you can make the tool entirely yours and ensure that it would be helpful even in the long run.

Have faith in your abilities

At a press conference, Larry Bird once said that a winner is a person who knows their God-given talents and works to turn them into skills and then uses them to accomplish his goals. The most successful businesspeople in the world are self –confident to the point of coming across as cocky or brash. Consider people like Bill Gates, Donald Trump, and Richard Branson. They have learned not to question their abilities.

Psychologists say one of the ways to become self-confident is to become competent (Kolbert, 2014). There is a straight line between becoming competent at what you do and positive thinking. You will find it easier to see the brighter side of things if you know that you do well at what you put your mind to do. The following are some tips to help you believe in your abilities:

- Focus on your strengths – You know the areas in which you are competent. The skills vary from person to person and from job to job. Pick yours and push yourself hard that you may become even better. You do not want to be mediocre.
- Let things go – It is okay to let some doors close. You cannot do everything, and it is wise not to try. If some things fall off your to-do list, you can delegate and

be purposeful in leaving some things out when you need to.

- Take care of yourself – How confident are you when you did not get enough sleep, are always exhausted, and have no energy? Eat right, sleep enough, hydrate, and exercise.
- Wake up early – The old adage 'early to bed, early to rise' is true. It did not earn its novelty without proving helpful. Many achievers wake up early to spend time meditating, reading, and working without distractions. You can get plenty done when you have some quiet time. Be sure to go to bed early as well.
- Brush up on your skills regularly – Most skills fade over time, more so in the technology and communications sector that is continuously upgrading. Do a

personal ROI by continually learning, taking refresher courses, and attending seminars where applicable.

Watch your thoughts

"Life is 10% what happens to you and 90% how you react." — Charles R. Swindoll

Reality is not neutral; you become what you think. You are always passing judgment on the things happening around you. Have you ever been in the same dangerous or risky situation as your friend? What differences did you notice in your responses? Where one helps to find a solution, another may scream and become confused. Where one rallies, another may become crippled with indecision. The point here is that your thoughts and your reality are unavoidably connected. When working to think positively, you have to be aware of this fact.

However, you have to be careful not to make it so simple that it goes against the very thing you are trying to achieve. Positive thinking is not just about the bright side; you have to embrace the whole self. Marcus Aurelius said of the soul that it becomes dyed with the color of the thoughts it has.

The society loves black and white statements that put you in one category and exempt you from another by default. When working to think positively, labels can be a burden.

Everyone has positive and negative thoughts and moments. It can be harmful to always pretend to be happy. If you focus just on one aspect, you will not see your blind spots. As an example, labeling yourself as a negative person could have you overplay your dramas and enter into self-pity.

Researchers say that optimists cope better with stress because they can handle adversity (Schmitz et. al., 2014) not because they always have a positive view. Their immune response is the same as that of pessimists. Positive thinking is not about making all things come true, but about handling all things like a master.

You can only do that if you are able to master yourself. Train yourself to treat your negative thoughts as suggestions from your brain rather than descriptions of who you are. This comes from understanding that there is nothing wrong with having negative emotions.

Positivity is not a status. It is a fluid state. Train your thoughts not to overplay just one aspect of a situation. The trick is to walk the taut line between optimism and pessimism as an observer.

As a rule of thumb, connect to the emotions you have so that you respond instead of react. This looks like not letting your preconceptions to shape how you behave but exploring your emotions so that you understand them. Feed wisdom and compassion instead of anger.

Think of positive thinking as an exercise in self-acceptance. Manage the strengths and flaws that you have to the point where you accept yourself as a person who makes mistakes but is also capable of doing great things. Positive thinking works only if you embrace the full reality of who you are.

Detox your mind
In the world today, attention is currency. The more attention people give something, the more valuable it becomes – the more exposure, the more profit. The more energy you give

something, the more it becomes powerful, and in a world that is always asking for your mental energy in emails to answer, clothing to wear, recipes to try, and ways to take photos, you have to guard your mind.

If you do not know what matters most to you, you can easily fall into patterns of anxiety. Unable to understand what deserves space, you can end up wasting your days in rabbit trails. Most people do not realize that you learn and grow from what you experience and absorb consistently. Detoxing your mind is about getting rid of the unnecessary things that make you feel burdened and stand in the way of you embracing a positive outlook on life.

The following are tips for detoxing your mind:

- Make a list of what to worry about

Have you ever noticed that if you have a plan for solving a problem, you no longer need to worry about it? The idea is simple; you do not worry about issues because you think rumination on them is productive. You worry about making sure you do not forget to deal with the issue because it is risky, or the threat it poses is huge.

Write everything down that bothers you in a 'to worry about' list. Set time aside so that you can review that list. You will find that most of the fears you have are unfounded, and you can make a plan to deal with the ones you can handle.

- Adopt junk journaling

Take a notebook and devote it only to things that you can classify as 'junk.' Keep the journal safe and private. Anytime you feel worked up, or your mind begins spinning, write everything down that comes to mind. Release the thoughts you have even if they do not make sense or you do not truly believe them.

- Spend time outside

Research has proven that when people spend more time in nature, they begin to see significant benefits to their health and wellness. Spending time in nature also allows you an easy way to gain clarity and to relax. You need that to put things into perspective.

- Unfollow those who do not add to your life

In a world where social media is almost a need, one can get caught up in a rabbit hole and find themselves without even realizing it in a cycle of comparisons and negative self-talk. Make a point of spending time filtering who you allow on your social media. If you spend time online, you might as well make it positive and productive. Assess who you follow regularly and ensure that every account you follow is actively adding to your life.

- Clean out old phone numbers

Everyone has some people that you know you will never speak to again or *should* never speak to again. It is part of being human. You want to allocate some time to delete any old phone numbers. This is not even about getting rid of temptation even if that could be part of it – bye, bye pesky ex – this is about the feeling you get after removing things you do not need. You will remember how far you have come, and everyone needs a dose of gratitude. It will also inject you with a sense of closure.

- Clear out your inbox

Your inbox should be like a 'to do' list. What is in your inbox every day should tell you what you need to attend to. Nothing is more stressful than fearing that you have lost important messages in your account because you do not have it cleaned out.

- Unsubscribe from unnecessary promotional information and emails

It could be that at one point you needed a service and you have outgrown it. Or perhaps, you subscribed to support a friend. Other times you even subscribe by mistake. Whatever the case, you may be prone to scrolling on websites every time you see a sale, and that could be eating into your time or expenses. As part of keeping your inbox clean and saving money and time, unsubscribe from anything you do not need. As a rule of thumb, set time to do a major cleaning of your inbox. From there, make a note to delete and unsubscribe from anything you do not want the first time you see it so that they do not pile up.

- Figure out the time you spend online

Research shows that many young people spend up to four hours online consuming content they do not even like. Imagine spending four hours every day, for two months, for example – assuming that you do not go online on weekends, which is highly unlikely; you spend up to seven days online in two months. It is tragic if that time is not spent doing productive things.

Download a browser extension to record how much time you spend online and on what sites you spend that time. Take an honest look at the number. There are also other downloadable apps on your phone that could track your time on social media. If that number is shocking to you, you know that it is time to change.

- Take a day off without photographs

You can live your life without having to document it. In today's era, it is possible to document and share all parts of your life online, which could expose you to security risks and could also introduce a pressure, making you feel like you have to constantly 'perform.' This may create undue stress, more so when you start making choices based on how you would appear to people instead of how the decisions would feel to you.

- Reflect on your life

If you did not know how your life looked to other people, how would you feel about it? Ask yourself this question honestly and find the areas of your life that you are genuinely happy with. Get rid of the parts you only enjoy because of the way they make you look to other people.

- Make it hard to sign in to social media

As earlier discussed, you can spend plenty of time mindlessly scrolling through social media. If you decide that that is not something you want any more for your life, you can make it more difficult to access social media accounts.

You can remove the auto-save option for your passwords, or you can delete the apps from your phone. Either way, make social media apps less accessible.

- Watch how you socialize

Personalities affect much of the way people socialize with others (Jung, 1921). A classic trait of ambiverts is that they are social and outgoing in some settings. This is a critical habit for anyone to develop regardless of where they fall on the extrovert – introvert scale. Be mindful of who you spend time with, what you share with them, who you connect with, and how you vent. This can affect your wellbeing, your life, and who you become.

- Remind yourself what the big picture is

What are your long-term goals? You want to set aside time to note what those goals are and call it a life vision. Reference this vision often and always have it in mind as you do the mundane tasks of life. It is easy to be caught up in the small details of life without knowing why. When you understand why, you can make supporting decisions that will lead you to your goal.

- Protect your mental space as much as you can

There is a common saying that asserts, 'There is nothing that enters a man from outside which can defile him, but the things which come out of him, those are the things that defile a man.' This idea is echoed in many sayings like 'do not judge a book by its cover' or 'still waters run deep.' Undeniably, what you let into your heart is what will make you the kind of person you become. If you are always listening to gossip, you will likely begin to enjoy no other form of conversation.

As part of de-cluttering your mind, be vigilant about protecting what you hear. Shift the conversation with friends who always gossip. Watch news selectively so that you do not stress yourself out with things you have no control over. The idea here is to commit to being the most peaceful and grounded person that you can be. Do not let just anything grab and keep your attention.

Shifting your mindset

At this point, if you have observed the tips on detoxing your mind, you have a lot of mental energy left to give to whatever it is that you choose. You will notice that you feel lighter. That is good. It means that you are headed in the right direction.

In life, change is inevitable, and you have to learn to accept it and maybe even anticipate it without making it a major mental hurdle. Chances are, as you did the suggested exercises, some things became clearer, and you realized things you do not need.

In this section, you will learn how to stay in this frame of mind with simple mental exercises. You do not want to slip back into mindless activities. It is a truth of today's generation that more people go through life mindlessly in one area or another. Shifting your mindset, in this case, refers to cementing some of the things you have learned about yourself as you detoxed your mind.

The following are things you can do:

- Meditate

Mindset is a muscle that can be improved upon and strengthened. One way to do this is to learn meditation. You do not have to be on the Alps with white garb and spend three months as a monk to learn how to do this. To get you started, when you find your thoughts wandering, remind yourself of the big picture you formulated. Mull over it and always find practical ways to make it a reality. You can commit to doing this for ten minutes a day for starters.

- Prioritize personal development

If you are reading this book, it says a lot about your composition and desire for change. You can zoom in on this desire. Making personal development a priority is about always pausing to find out where you are in life and the changes you need to make. Self-inquiry is at the heart of this.

- Notice three positive changes every day

Dopamine is a feel-good neurotransmitter that the brain releases when you engage in activities like sex or other enjoyable things. It contributes to feelings of satisfaction or pleasure as part of the reward system. You can make sure you enjoy such feelings every day by noticing three changes in your life that are a result of your efforts. However small, make an effort to note them, and you will retrain your brain for growth.

- Write a post-mortem

Positive emotions are excellent and propelling, but sometimes you need something to run away from so that you can keep yourself moving forward. The idea here is to imagine the worst-case scenario for your life. Do not play about with it. Ask yourself what you can imagine to be the worst possible future for yourself and spell it out. Once you realize how simple it is for a person to mess up their life, you will be quick to embrace change.

- Imagine the inevitable

"The only certainty in life is death" – Benjamin Franklin.

There is wisdom in occasionally contemplating death and imagining what kind of legacy you would like to leave. Once you know that this life is fleeting, you can position yourself to make changes instead of being stagnant when you encounter something you do not like. Imagine for a minute that you were writing your eulogy; what would you want to be said about you? If you find that 'he was a kind man' is something you would desire, use that as a springboard. On days you feel less than motivated, ask yourself what you would do differently if you learned that this was the last day of your life, and then do that.

- Enhance your inner work

Earlier in the book, it was mentioned that self-acceptance has one of the foundational truths of positive thinking. Inner work is a pillar of self-acceptance. Inner work is the spiritual and psychological practice of diving deep into your inner self for the purpose of self-exploration, self-understanding, healing, and transformation.

Every person has some things about them that they could improve. It is easy to demand that people accept you for who you are, and there is a sense to which loved ones must do this, but successful people are those who learn to master themselves.

To do this, listen to trusted loved ones. They may not know you the way you know yourself, but their outsider perspective can help you to understand what areas to focus on to lead you out of the 'mental quicksand.' Be honest with yourself, and you will begin to see the results.

Inner work also goes beyond listening to your loved ones (Johnson, 1986). It is about illuminating your hidden feelings, thoughts, memories, beliefs, wounds, prejudices, shadows, and other emotional or mental conditions that influence your ability to feel whole at your core. Doing inner work is about moving past your limitations, fears, addictions, loneliness, depressions, and feelings of un-wholeness that are common to human beings but unique to each person, their experiences, and perception of the world.

The following are some signs you need to enhance inner work:

- You feel lost
- You have people-pleasing tendencies
- You do not know who you are
- You feel like an outsider in the world no matter how hard you try
- Life feels unreal
- You are not confident being who you are
- You frequently get into fights

- You are constantly unmotivated
- You have low self-esteem
- You feel a sense of hopelessness
- You have fits of intense sadness or anger
- You struggle to trust other people
- You self-sabotage
- You feel a sense of emptiness
- You are unable to sleep properly
- You keep attracting the wrong people in your life
- You keep repeating mistakes
- You have many and strong emotional triggers
- You get easily obsessive and neurotic

Ideally, everyone should assess their inner work two or three times a year to recalibrate, stay on track, and get rid of any emotional baggage they may have picked up along the way. The more signs you relate with, the more it points to a need to do inner work first.

Think of this practice as a foundational principle for positive thinking. It is akin to digging deep into the ground when building a house so that it stands firm. Thereafter, think of it as maintenance.

Accept that change happens

Three things are true for every person regardless of their situation in life: time is precious, life is short, and your ego always needs some humility. Whether it is an innovative idea or a business venture, the nature of life is evolution. Change is as natural as oxygen. You need to accept that. You need to recognize also that change will happen with your help or without it, and you get to choose which option it will be.

If you want to make sure that you are party to the changes happening in your life and around you, be vulnerable and open to those around you, and accept their help with discretion.

Accepting change is the path of least resistance, but sometimes it may not be the best path. Only a community can help you to understand when to let go and when to resist. You do not need to let everyone you meet in, but if you accept the thoughts of other people you value, you not only shift your mindset, but you also become a better person in whatever capacity you have to operate.

Get rid of the 'sunken cost mindset.' This is the idea that you have invested so much time in something and so you need to stay attached to it. Sometimes walking away or pivoting is the better decision. Do not allow the fear of losing your investments be what guides your choices. Think rationally about what you get from continuing down a path or going a new direction.

Summary

Nurture your mind with great thoughts, for you will never go any higher than you think." – Benjamin Disraeli

Let's recap the things you have learned by this point:

Positive thinking is a bit more than a fad. For it to be successful, you have to think of it as an exercise in changing who you are at your core in some ways. It is about:

- o Knowing yourself
- o Having faith in your abilities

Positive Mindset Mastery

- Watching your thoughts
- Detoxing your mind
- Shifting your mindset
- Accepting that change happens

Positive Mindset Mastery

Chapter 2: The Power of Positive Thinking

The History

The term 'positive thinking' has been in use for a while, but few people know where it comes from. It has religious roots, but it does not come from one religion. Positive thinking has evolved from all religions of the world through a new thought movement. One Harvard professor and psychologist wrote about the movement when writing about the varieties of religious experience. He referred to it as the religion of a healthy mind saying that the most significant discovery of his generation was that man could change his life by changing the attitude of his mind.

New thought originated in Europe in the 1700s, and then later, Ralph Waldo Emerson introduced it to the United States. He focused on perception, saying that moods, temperaments, and thoughts color reality. In a famous essay, he wrote that temperament is the 'iron wire on which you string beads' (Emerson, 1841). He said that life is about moods arranged like beads in a string and that people pass through them, proving to have many lenses to paint their world their hue.

It was not enough to talk about truth, according to Emerson. Words alone could never make people see their own temperament. In his preaching, Emerson stirred people up and inspired a different breed of poets and writers who subscribe to the new thought.

There are countless examples of people who have done amazing things based on changing how they view life. A Hindu guru, Swami Vivekananda, founded the Vedanta society at the height of the positive thinking movements. The common thread with all the examples is the power of thought. Everyone agrees that 'whatever you think, so are you.'

The Present

The power of positive thinking is remarkable. You may still believe that the idea that your mind could change your world is too good to be true, but be assured that there is a lot of good you derive from thinking positively.

Before getting into the nitty-gritty of changing

how you think, can you guess the things the most successful people think about all day every day?

It is simple: healthy and happy people mull over the things they want and how to get them. When you consider and talk about the things you want and how to get them, you feel more in control of your life and happier. You trigger your brain to release endorphins that directly improve your mood and, consequently, your perception.

Optimism

Psychological tests show that happy people appear to have a unique quality that makes them live a better life than the average person. They are optimistic. The best news about it is that you can learn to be optimistic. It's a mindset.

By the law of cause and effect, if you say and do what other happy and healthy people with a positive attitude say and do, you will soon become one of them, see the same results, and have similar experiences.

Optimists have a way of seeing things differently as they interact with the world. They keep their minds on the things they want and ways to get it. Their goals are clear, and they are confident that they will get to them eventually. Optimists also try to find the good in every situation or problem. It is a truth universally acknowledged that if you are looking for something beneficial or good in a situation or a person, you will ultimately find it.

Optimists also look to find the lesson in every failure or setback. Instead of blaming other people and getting upset, they control their emotions. They ask the question, what can I learn from this experience? Emotion control is a major aspect of positive thinking, which is why it gets a chapter of its own later in the book.

You can decide today that you will develop a positive attitude toward yourself and a positive way of thinking about your life and the people around you. From there, you have to train your mind to focus on one thought at a time until you form neural pathways that establish new habits.

It is difficult to change your way of thinking in the heat of the moment when emotions are running high. In one sense, positive thinking is about a decision you make in advance. You have to decide that whatever comes at you, you will strive to respond positively. You will look to help as opposed to making things worse.

As a general rule, happy people are grateful for what they have in life instead of complaining or worrying about what they do not have.

Assume that people around you mean well. Most people are decent and are doing the best that they know how to. Look for the good in their actions and words, and you will surely find it in the words they tell you or in the ways they choose to behave. With that as a background, resolve that you will be cheerful regardless of the circumstance.

In actuality, it is easy to be cheerful when things go as you plan, but what about when you are dealing with challenges and setbacks?

After learning how to think positively, you will start to notice many exciting changes in your environment. Your brain will start running on endorphins that will boost your confidence, and you will feel more capable of meeting challenges and doing greater things outside of your comfort zone. How then do you do that?

10 Ps for Reprogramming Your Mind

In one way or another, most people are not living the life of their dreams and may have settled into the status quo.

If you have a vague idea of the things you think you deserve and are feeling frustrated because you veered off the path, you can use the discontentment as fuel to reprogram your mind and change. Discontentment, though, is double-edged. Without proper handling, your frustration could sabotage your potential instead of helping it. Most people will work hard for a few days and then revert to their old ways instead of making a lasting change.

Controlling your mind and redirecting your focus on making the life you want is a sure way to make sure you live a life that will give you passion, joy, and fulfillment. Your brain is meant to regulate and reinforce your life.

There is a homeostatic impulse in your mind that regulates functions like breathing, heartbeat, and temperature. Through that autonomic nervous system, the homeostatic impulse maintains a balance of brain chemicals and helps your body function in harmony most times. What you may not realize is that your brain is meant to regulate your physical self and tries to regulate your mental self as well. It is continuously bringing things to your attention and filtering others out. No wonder you may encounter stimuli to reaffirm your existing beliefs. Psychologists refer to this as confirmation bias. You may then have repeated impulses and thoughts which mirror and mimic the things you did in the past.

In that sense, your subconscious acts as a gatekeeper for your comfort zone. It is the realm where you stay habitually and represents everything you expect and the actions you routinely build and reinforce. When you want to change your way of doing things, whether it is in just one area or a complete change, here are a few tips:

1. Prepare for unobvious change

Often when people talk about positive thinking, they make the connection between thinking positively and the belief that you have the ability to do something. While that is true, the first step to creating a significant change is not believing it to be possible, but being willing to see if it could be.

You cannot expect to make the jump from a full-on skeptic to a totally sold out believer. The step into being open to the possibilities is a major one at the beginning. Perhaps you are trying to do a task you have been postponing for months, or maybe it is a scary email proposition you need to send. Whatever the case, the first step to reprogramming your mind is seeing if you are willing to see the change you hope for as a possibility.

2. Permit yourself to succeed

Rather than regurgitating the old story that has kept you from doing the task at hand in the first place, you can change your inner monologue to something like, 'I allow my life to be good.'

Permit yourself to be successful and happy without feeling guilty about it. Most people will find that they have associations between being dishonorable or corrupt and success. If you are one such person, you may need to work harder than you expect. Consider the chapter on managing emotions.

3. Process other people's fears

Have you ever told your friend news you found exciting, and they responded with a simple, 'oh'? Sometimes what feels to you to be a feat could be unimpressive in the eyes of another person. Part of reprogramming your mind is remembering that people's fears are projections of whatever their situations are. They say nothing to your capability. When you encounter such fears, sit with them and process them in a journal, for example, and then let them go.

4. Positively reinforce yourself

Positive reinforcement could be anything that works for you. It could be a champagne bottle in the fridge for celebrations, or it could be making your morning alarm call to congratulate you. The idea here is to make sure that whatever you touch brings hopefulness and positivity. You can even keep post-it notes in your mirror or computer – whatever improves your perception of your worth is worth doing.

5. Profess your present success

It may be a bit of a stretch to say statements like 'I am a CEO' or 'I own a yacht' before they are a reality. Still, you do want to start speaking about the things you want out of life and not in terms of something to do in the future. Rather than saying, 'I hope to accomplish this...' say instead that, 'I am working towards this...' Do not make the mistake of thinking that you will be happy when you meet your goal, but strive for happiness as you work towards it.

6. Perfect your vision space

Earlier in the book, you learned to create a life goal and to keep it in mind. On this point, you want to write it on paper and have it somewhere you can easily see it. Whether it is a Pinterest board, a notebook, a blog, or words in a journal, you want a representation of your goal to bring up whenever you need some more motivation.

7. Pinpoint your resistance

Your subconscious will sometimes hold you back because you have conflicting beliefs. To identify your beliefs, answer the questions highlighted under the chapter on mastering your emotions. Find a way to meet the needs that cause you to procrastinate before you move forward.

8. Plan your life

This point is set separately from your vision space because there is more to it. It is difficult to make an accurate ten-year plan. Things keep changing over time. For example, before you learn a new skill, you could only be qualified for two jobs. After learning, you are eligible for five more, and your options increase. The better you become in one aspect, the more likely that you will have more and better choices.

Planning your life is about identifying your motivations and your core values. What ultimate goal do you want to meet while you are alive? What legacy do you want to leave behind? These are the things that should guide every decision you make in life.

9. Present your requests

Ask for the things you want, even if there is a chance of being denied. If you are looking for a promotion in your workplace, sit with your boss and announce your intentions. Reach out to other companies. Begin asking for the things you want, and eventually, you will start to get them.

10. Proceed with the flow

Your job is to focus on the 'what' and not get

caught up on the 'how.' If you want, for example, to be able to run your business remotely, rather than giving up when your first attempt fails, reimagine other ways to achieve that vision that are more financially lucrative.

The point is that you cannot predict life – it will surprise you the way things get accomplished. Rather than obsessively attaching to all the details working out as you expect they should, open yourself to the possibilities and potential even if they present ideas you never thought of before.

Positive energy

You have probably heard this phrase in the world of social media often used interchangeably with 'positive vibes.' It is all about controlling the things you think about. You create and experience different kinds of energies that affect the way you feel and what you do. Some energies are powerful and easy to recognize, and others are subtle and intuitively felt. It is fair to say that everything you sense is energy.

The things that you think, say, and do, even the things you do not do, produce an energy that will affect you and those around you. If you concentrate on producing positive energy, you will begin to see your life improve, and you will touch more lives than you ever imagined.

So what exactly is energy?

Think of energy as anything that will invoke a reaction inside you – if it makes you react, feel, ponder, or tick, that is energy. It comes to people in different forms. The seat you take in the morning, the music you choose to listen to, and the book you are just starting to read all provoke some reaction inside of you.

Consider music; how does your favorite kind make you feel? What energy do you get from it? If you are still not clued in on what energy is about, take out your music player and play a song you like. Take a break from reading this book, close your eyes, and pay attention to the song as it plays. What do you feel?

Music is among the most easily recognizable and powerful forms of energy. No wonder it formed the basis of many traditions. An excellent musician has the ability to create sensations in the audience.

If you want to shift your energy quickly, music is one of the easiest ways. Athletes will often listen to songs before they go to play to channel their adrenaline; artists often play music to get "in the zone," and many writers will rely on music in their writing process.

However, even though music is the simplest way to explain the concept, it is not the only way to get energized.

Some people wake up, swing open the curtains, and allow the sun in as the first thing and draw energy from that. Other people run to coffee. On the reverse, some people find rain to have the potential to affect their mood negatively, so they find it beneficial to practice mindfulness when it is raining.

The most important thing about feeling positive energy is being fully present. When you are in the moment, you will be able to respond in ways that are truly you and that propel you forward.

Still, it may not be as simple as A-B-C-D. To help obtain positive energy, you can make a list of everything that makes you feel good and use it as a basis for the things to do when your mood is off. If you find that being in nature gives you that energy, you can try spending some more time in the outdoors. If the sun does that for you, there is a chance that animals, trees, and flowers will do the same. This is discussed further in the chapter on daily rituals.

The benefits

Positive energy is contagious. If you are the kind of person that emits positivity and zeal, the outer world will begin to notice.

Do you know of people that everyone likes to be around? These are people who radiate alluring energy all the time, and everyone loves to feed off that energy. They make other people smile with their stories and with their attitudes.

It is indeed challenging to keep positive energy flowing in an unwaveringly cynical world.

The unpredictability of life often causes people to have volatile emotions. Everyone experiences emotional ups and downs as life unfolds. If you do not know how to process those experiences, you will leave some emotions unresolved in an emotional bypass. For example, one of the driving ideas of positive energy is the ability and the space to process emotion and deal with it in healthy ways, before you are consumed by it. It assumes that while your circumstances can change at any time and have a degree of mystery to them, your inner world does not have to be the same.

If your ability to deal with the stresses of

everyday life is underdeveloped, you run the risk of having a negative outlook on life by default. Undoubtedly, negativity will manifest as stress, and when you are stressed, you put yourself at risk emotionally, mentally, and physically. To counteract stress and thus the negative energy, you have to be proactive in understanding your thoughts and behaviors that cause the negative cycle.

Positive energy will bring you the following benefits:

- Improving your relationships

Relationships are a vital part of life. If they are strong, they will strengthen you and can make you more energetic and happier. Relationships with a strong bond based on positivity will often last the longest and will serve you the best.

- Becoming a more spiritual person

Positivity supports your spirituality. Spiritual people believe in something higher than themselves as they go through life. They draw strength from spiritual connectivity and faith. Studies show that spiritual people are mentally stronger and cope with stress better.

- Unleashing your creativity

Positive energy will boost your creativity. It will make you more likely to find innovative solutions to your problem. Some famous people say that their positivity kept them going because it encouraged them to think outside the box. Your solution-finding becomes child-like.

- Feeling more relaxed

Stress can harm your body and mind. It takes away your energy and puts you on edge. Boosting your positive energy will make you relax and equip you to deal with the difficulties that come your way.

- Improving your sleep

Positive energy has both physical and mental benefits. According to a study that looked to understand the relationship between sleep and positivity, researchers found that positivity helps a person to sleep soundly. It lessens insomnia related to stress. Negative people are prone to worry, and worry eats at your mind at times when you are supposed to be resting. If you can sleep well, your immune system will run better; you will have better heart health, breathing, and lower blood pressure, all of which contribute to a better quality of life.

- Improving productivity

Positivity will give you the energy you need to do the things you need to do. Fear can steal from your strength and negatively influence your productivity. Positive energy will unburden your mind to make you feel ready to tackle whatever comes your way.

- Giving you an attitude of gratitude

Positive energy will boost your general view of life. Researchers say that a happy attitude almost always leads to a happy life. Positive energy helps to take a step back and see the blessings you have in life and to be grateful for them.

- Being a better role model

If you are a parent, you know that nothing

would make you happier than to see your children become successful and mature adults. Positive energy will help you model the kind of life you would want your kids to lead one day. They will see the way you handle difficulties, and they will learn from you.

- Improving self-confidence

Positive energy is inevitably tied to self-confidence. It will strengthen your resolve to deal with the difficult things in life. It will help you to fight fear, which can be paralyzing when you want to try new things.

The roadblocks and how to overcome them

Everyone can enjoy the benefits of positive thinking, but not everyone manages to. The following are some of the roadblocks that could get in the way and how you can overcome them:

- Letting success dictate your life

It is normal to desire success, and that is not negative behavior. However, the obsessive preoccupation with that success, which then commands and directs your life, is unhealthy. This is the reason many successful people are miserable.

Allowing society to influence what success means to you is toxic. Society is often consumer-based and materialistic, and so its definition of success may be based on how much money you have in your bank account, the home you live in, and the car you drive. This definition does not allow for the uniqueness of individuality.

To address this, you have to re-define what success means to you and keep your focus on your life vision and what truly brings you happiness. Envision what a successful life looks like to you and resolve to live it without letting outside influences in.

- Preoccupation with self-image or vanity

Joan Rivers, a very talented comedian, actress, and television host, was famously known for being obsessed with the way she looked and underwent more than 730 plastic surgeries in her life. She continued with the procedures until she died at 81.

You may not think of yourself as someone who would go to such an extent but think about it. In what ways have you bought into the society's definitions of beauty – expensive makeup, makeovers, toned bodies, fancy hairstyles, and designer clothes? Most young people will find themselves susceptible to these influences. You can see this in disorders like anorexia and bulimia, which often lead to depression and even suicide.

Trying to be accepted and to improve your self-image by going by what society calls beauty will prove empty. True beauty can only be found in your mind, heart, and soul. Recognize and love yours.

- Addiction to stress

Believe it or not, studies have shown that some people are addicted to stress.

"We wear our stress like a badge of honor, humble-bragging about how little sleep we got

last night, how our weekend was spent racing to meet a deadline, and how we're too busy to take a vacation." – Nuwer, Rachel (2014)

The psychological repercussions of ongoing stress include headaches, increased heart rate, asthma, obesity, depression, and diabetes, among others.

Stress addiction does not come from external circumstances but your internalization of stress. The solution to this is deep breathing, guided imagery, and meditation. Practice the daily morning and evening rituals discussed in the final chapter if you are prone to this.

- Worrying about the mundane in life

I recently stumbled across an interesting post on social media: "Imagine if you had $86,400 in your account, and someone stole $10 from you. Would you be upset and throw away the remaining $86,390 in hopes of getting back at the person who took your $10? Or would you just move on and live? We all have 86,400 seconds each day. Don't let someone's negative 10 seconds ruin your remaining 86,390."

It is annoying to run five minutes late for a meeting, and it's an inconvenience to forget your cell phone at home. However, these are not significantly life-changing issues. Why would you allow them to derail your mood?

It is alright to get irritated when the small and unpleasant event happens, but do not become overindulgent. You are merely wasting time and energy on situations that are insignificant and trivial. It can lead to unwarranted stress and anxiety. Don't sweat the small stuff. Let thoughts fade before they become a negative mindset.

- Living in the past

Regardless of the severity and number of mistakes you've made in the past, every day is a second chance. It is impossible to live in the moment when you continuously replay and reflect on the past. Continually replaying the mistakes of the past will condition your brain to always expect the worst. It becomes counterproductive to the future and the present, and you begin to feel burdened and victimized.

There are times it may be hard to just 'forget and move on,' especially if you experienced trauma, but it is not impossible. Consider meditation and journaling to help you in the process of healing.

- Possessiveness in your relationships

When you are possessive, you cling tightly to people and relationships, saying 'mine!' Possessiveness is a sure sign of fear and insecurity. It could be coming from conditioning, but possessiveness harms you and your loved ones. It breeds problems like loneliness, anxiety, sadness, and anger, which compromise your sense of understanding and peace. More often than not, it yields a result opposite to what you want – disconnection from your loved ones.

The first step to dealing with possessiveness is thinking of protecting the people you care for from yourself. Everyone needs freedom and space to make choices that are good for them.

Accept that fact and realize that distance may actually strengthen the relationship.

- Unforgiveness

Forgiveness is often considered the first step to healing. Unfortunately, some people nurse grudges for long periods. That unrelenting bitterness will cause anger and resentment to build, which will ultimately disrupt your positive energy. It will make it harder to manage your emotions and establish healthy relationships.

To deal with this, remember that when you forgive someone, it is as much about you as it is about them. Let go, and you will be able to embrace gratitude, joy, hope, and peace. You will lessen the psychological and emotional impact of the hurt. Forgiveness will not excuse or justify their actions, but it will help you to make peace.

- Judging others

There are times you may judge someone's motive from merely looking at them. On the one hand, not judging others can be counterproductive and harmful – it is reasonable to evaluate and observe others to know how to conduct yourself around them. On the other hand, judging others could be damaging when specific feelings or thoughts cause resentment.

When you have a negative perception, you will likely become dismissive or hostile. When you start to feel this way, remind yourself of the path you are walking and ask yourself questions like: Why do I judge them? Do I understand how they think? Can I be empathetic in this situation? Do I know what they are dealing with?

Summary

In this chapter, you have learned that positive thinking is not just a fad that began yesterday. Its roots trace far back into history. In deciding to embrace a positive mindset, you have decided to join a community of many highly regarded people in history. You have also chosen a healthier life with the numerous benefits of having a positive mindset.

Practice the ten **P's** to reprogram your mind. **P**repare for change, **P**ermit yourself to be happy, **P**rocess your emotions, **P**ositively reinforce yourself, remembering that you are your biggest fan, and **P**rofess your beliefs. As you do so, make sure that your vision is **P**erfect and that you have **P**inpointed what often gets in your way. **P**lan your life according to your core values, **P**resent your requests to the right people and **P**roceed with the flow.

You will soon see yourself dealing with the challenges of living better. When you encounter problems, as you inevitably will, come back to the section on roadblocks and find out how to overcome things like:

- Judging others
- Unforgiveness
- Possessiveness in relationships
- Stress addiction
- Living in the past and
- Worrying about the mundane in life

Positive Mindset Mastery

Positive Mindset Mastery

Chapter 3: Inferiority Complex and Self-Doubt

Everyone, at some point, questions their abilities. Even though it is distressing, it is normal that one would wonder whether they measure up to other people. It is also reasonable to momentarily feel incompetent for maybe performing less than you expected or for not being as well-situated in life as others.

However, those feelings of insufficiency and insecurity are supposed to be occasional or situational. When they arise, you may brood over them for a short while and then move on by reminding yourself that you have other strengths. Even when a major event causes a flare in self-doubt, you would preferably find ways to feel secure, engaged, and productive.

This is often harder for people who have an inferiority complex. This is an old-fashioned term for chronic low self-esteem. People with an inferiority complex will not bounce back as quickly. You may lament your shortcomings, call yourself names, and criticize yourself harshly, attacking your self-esteem when it is most fragile. The cycle can be so deep that it holds you back professionally and personally.

People who have low self-esteem tend to get very little because they expect little. It becomes a self-fulfilling divination, so as disappointments mount, you become more vulnerable and discouraged, and you become biased against yourself. Consequently, you reinforce the feelings of being 'less than' in many aspects of life – physically, intellectually, psychologically, and socially.

The good news is that there are things you can do to deal with the unhealthy responses and to get over the psychological distress that may stand in the way of you being positive. There are ways to build your self-esteem. Before considering those, let's discuss what inferiority complex looks like:

How Inferiority Complex Presents

Having the assurance that Usain Bolt would outrun you in a sprint is not the same as having a feeling of being inferior. An inferiority complex is the constant and unyielding feeling that you have to measure up to everyone else.

It is ungrounded in reality, because all you know is that you do not measure up, but you cannot identify why.

Inferiority complex or low-self-esteem is a generalized feeling of inadequacy whose basis is not rational judgment.

The following is a list of emotions that people with a low self-esteem commonly experience:

- Helplessness and hopelessness – These are critical emotions for someone who is depressed as well. You feel that no matter what you do, you cannot be as good as you should be or as other people appear to be. Regardless of how well you do it, it will not be good enough. It is common for some high achievers to still feel like they are failures.

- Anxiety – In this case, you fear being unmasked or found out to be inadequate. It may also have a sense of imposter syndrome even when you are doing well in different areas of life.
- Resentment, defensiveness, and envy – You can experience envy, resentment, and defensiveness so frequently that you become unable to tell them apart. They sometimes accompany guilt.

My friend, Caroline, often said that she felt 'ugly.' Objectively speaking, she was not, but that did not matter. Felling ugly and being ugly can be disconnected. In that frame of mind, evidence of the objective perception of others is often rejected and rationalized away – it has to be so that the inferiority complex protects itself.

Caroline then continues to rehearse the narrative that she is not good enough. She soon finds it hard to be specific even though she tries to articulate her feelings and where they come from. Where do you think her inferiority complex came from?

Think about this example as you read the rest of this chapter and try to answer it at the end based on what you learn.

History of the Inferiority Complex

The APA (American Psychological Association) defines the term 'inferiority complex' as the basic feeling of insecurity and inadequacy one feels from imagined or actual psychological or physical deficiencies.

The term was coined in 1907 by an influential psychoanalyst Alfred Adler. He used it to explain why many people do not have the motivation to do what is in their best interests and to pursue the goals they have in life.

Contemporary psychologists, psychiatrists, and mental health professionals use the term interchangeably with low self-esteem.

Symptoms and Signs of Inferiority Complex

As earlier mentioned, it is human nature to sometimes feel inferior, but the key is in how you respond to those feelings.

Do the feelings of inferiority motivate you to try and do better and to learn? They should. Or do they cause you to shut down and distrust? Worse still, do you get jealous of other people and put them down to make yourself feel better? Do you blame others for things you should work to change? When patterns like these become consistent in many circumstances, you may have an inferiority complex.

It will show up as a collection of negative feelings, thoughts, tendencies, and behaviors. The following are signs to look out for:

- Perfectionism

In this case, one overcompensates to make up for whatever makes them feel inadequate. A person could try to achieve more and to be perfect in whatever they do. Sometimes, they become cocky as they present their achievements to the point where they sound narcissistic.

- You prefer fading into the background

Inferiority complex is closely linked to avoidant behavior. For example, you feel comfortable being overlooked, or you avoid stepping up in social situations because you are afraid of being rejected. It could get to the place where other people notice your discomfort with yourself.

- Sensitivity to criticism

People with low self-esteem are incredibly susceptible to the thoughts of others and will take offense even when it is unintended. Any kind of criticism or critique is held and ruminated over. They will not respond kindly to jokes or teasing at their expense, and when they feel disrespected, they take out aggression on others to intimidate them and to reduce the feelings of being attacked.

- Fault finding

When you have low self-esteem, you may make a habit of finding other people's faults. You tend to be more critical of other people. If a friend appears to be more successful than you are, you may look down on their career path instead of being happy for them. Some people even take it further still, bullying others and putting them down consistently.

- You only like yourself when you outshine others

Comparison is human nature, but there are unhealthy and healthy ways to deal with it. The healthy way is to focus on making yourself a better person. If you have an inferiority complex, you focus on being better than others.

- You do not believe other people's compliments

If you have low self-esteem, people's comments about your strengths ring false. It is worth noting that most self-esteem issues come from childhood and family relationships, a factor that will be discussed later in the chapter on managing relationships.

- You assume the worst too fast

Being pessimistic is defined as tending to see the worst aspect of things or believing that the worst will happen. If you notice that you blow others off for the smallest of reasons, it may be a sign that you have some issues to work through. For example, if a date cancels a dinner date but gives a good reason, you may still refuse to go on another date because you think they are not attracted to you. Sometimes when people give up too fast, they have an inferiority complex and may be leaving for the sake of ego.

Other signs include:

- Continually focusing on upsetting thoughts
- Withdrawing from family members, coworkers, and colleagues
- Shutting down because of embarrassment, shame, guilt, and helplessness
- Taking responsibility for the failures and shortcomings of others
- Seeking validation or attention by faking depression, sickness
- Avoiding any competition where efforts may be compared

An inferiority complex not only hurts you but hurts the people around you as well. The good news is that you do not have to live with it.

Risk Factors and Causes of Inferiority Complex

Before providing corrective actions, it is crucial to understand the root of the problem so that it addressed adequately.

Research suggests that the psychological and behavioral characteristics associated with low self-esteem come from the following factors:

- Genetics

Genetic research has found that people inherit variations in the receptor for oxytocin, the hormone responsible for positive emotions. Some variations cause people to feel less optimistic and to have low self-esteem as well as low personal mastery.

- Family environment

Early caregivers have a significant impact on whether your genetic tendencies toward self-doubt are softened or made worse. A child whose parent is highly critical may internalize their words and carry them into adulthood. During early childhood, you are the most impressionable, and if you face constant criticism, there is a high likelihood that you will grow to feel inferior, powerless, and insecure. The great Greek philosopher Aristotle once said, "Give me a child until he is 7, and I will show you the man."

- Society

There are unrealistic standards all over the place, from social media, advertisers, authority figures, and celebrities that could easily reinforce perceptions about yourself and cause self-doubt. Society is always bombarding you with messages on how to behave, what you should own by a specific age, the size of body that is ideal, the color of hair you should have, and the type of items like cars that is ideal. The messaging is sometimes subliminal. Without realizing it, you could internalize those messages, and they become an internal judge. You start to feel diminished to the point where you deem yourself unworthy.

A general characteristic across all types of people with low self-esteem is that they compare themselves with other people in unhealthy ways. In a world where you will constantly be told to buy things because of their value while you are force-fed a diet of perfection, it is easy for the inferiority complex to become worse. It is often said that it is what is on the inside that matters most. Still, society is more centered around celebrating someone's fame, wealth, car, or bodyweight superficially.

What makes it worse sometimes is that society seems to say one thing and do another, and so when you find yourself feeling less than because you have less, you give in to shame rather than working to better yourself. Shame only compounds the problem.

Part of adopting a positive mindset is knowing when to reject the lie. It is about self-objectivity in considering your shortcomings and working for their improvement. It is not using those shortcomings as a way to define oneself as Caroline in the original example did. It is not about despising oneself. It's about learning self-love, supporting, and encouraging yourself.

What then do you do with your inferiority complex?

Dealing with an Inferiority Complex

1. Face the emotional memories

Often, if you have an inferiority complex, you have many unhappy feelings that will fuel your thoughts. With this step, examine your thoughts. You can practice journaling with prompts to help you to widen your perspective and to challenge your thoughts. Sometimes you make a conclusion based on one emotionally charged event that is not true across all similar situations. For example, a heartbroken girl may conclude that all men are players when, in fact, every situation is different, and the next guy she meets may very well be the man of her dreams. Journaling will help you to unpack situations and gain perspective on them.

If your feelings are strong, it is advisable to face them head-on. Once you do, your thoughts will naturally become more moderate and manageable.

As an exercise, hone in on the feeling you encounter most that you do not want to have anymore. Close your eyes and access it. If it produces any specific memory where the feeling was shared, that is a memory you need to process.

Also note, it may be challenging to do this exercise the first few times, but once you push through, the impact of the feeling lessens, and the memories keep getting less painful. You can do this exercise with a loved one you trust, but be sure to let them in on what you are doing before you start.

- Be yourself

In the famous words of Oscar Wilde, 'Be yourself, everyone else is already taken' (1890). The best thing you can do in life is to accept who you are and try to be the best version of yourself possible.

The moment that you stop caring what others think about you will become the moment that you're free. One of the things that cripple people is wanting to be like and live like someone else. To do that is to leave behind what makes you unique. You cannot impersonate a person and be true to yourself. It will not make you happy to replicate someone else's life. This is not to say that you cannot learn from other people or have role models.

However, having other people inspire you means that you assimilate some traits they have into yourself. It does not mean that you want the exact life they have. The inferiority complex will thrive when you try to be someone you are not.

- Be specific

Sometimes all you need is to acknowledge whatever it is that makes you feel inferior. What are you inferior about?

Emotional thinking often blows things out of proportion. Being specific helps you to identify how your thinking is inconsistent with logic. Ask yourself questions that would help to clarify your feelings. For example, of all the people in the world, which ones make you feel inferior? Why?

You may find that you are intimidated by rich people, academic people, good-looking people, or accomplished people. From there, keep zooming in and figure out whether you are being too selective with the people you choose to compare yourself to.

- Dare to live differently

"The only dare you ever want to take is the dare to be all that you can be." – Catherine Pulsifer

Most people are prisoners to the opinions of others. People are too scared to be themselves. Life is not as restrictive as it was in the past when the only choices a person had were those presented in their village or town. Now, thanks to technology, the options for careers have changed. People are working remotely for employers they have never met. You can wear your hair long or short, and you would be called trendy instead of an outcast. Even what is considered proper official dressing has changed. Many traditional norms have been cast aside. You now have more freedoms than ever before.

The question to ask yourself here is, what do you want to do? Do not worry that it sounds out of the box, and do not tie yourself to what you think you are supposed to do.

- Get rid of the utopian assumptions

Most of the time, when you are feeling inferior, you have all-or-nothing thinking. Utopianism is about regret and a fanciful reality. It's the **'if only...'** thoughts that continuously run through our minds. Many people make the mistake of thinking that they would be happier **if only** they were more attractive, or earned more, or had more things going for them.

Life does not work that way. It is possible that you could be more confident by losing 20 pounds. However, what makes people feel inferior is often more deeply rooted, and achieving the goal may not meet the need. It could leave you wanting more. The goal is to learn to be content and grateful as a human being.

Everyone has deep needs. We long to be loved, to connect, to be useful, and to grow. These needs have to be met to live a life that is fulfilling.

Summary

This chapter zoomed in on inferiority complex and how it stands in the way of a positive mindset. You learned what low self-esteem looks like, how it presents itself, the risk factors, and the causes, and you were equipped to deal with it.

When an inferiority complex rears its ugly head:

- Be specific with your emotions to clarify them
- Eliminate the utopian assumptions
- Face the emotional memories
- Be yourself and
- Dare to live differently!

Chapter 4: Managing Your Emotions

What Are Emotions?

It may sound like a simple question, but it is essential to define what 'emotions' mean in this chapter to understand how it applies to your life and the attitude with which you confront situations.

Different types of those emotions rule your day. You make decisions based on whether you are sad, bored, happy, angry, or frustrated. You choose hobbies and activities based on how they make you feel. It makes sense that you would want to understand them as they can influence how you live life.

According to psychologist Don Hockenbury, emotion is a complicated psychological state that involves three distinct components: a subjective experience, a physiological response, and a behavioral or expressive response (1997).

In 1972, a psychologist suggested six basic emotions to be universal, including surprise, disgust, fear, sadness, anger, and happiness (Eckman, 1972). In 1999, the list was expanded to include satisfaction, excitement, embarrassment, pride, shame, contempt, and amusement.

Scientists have agreed on the major elements

of emotions:

- The subjective experience

Experts believe that, universally, people experience some basic emotions, but the experience can be subjective. All anger, for example, is not the same. It can range from blinding rage to mild annoyance. Since emotions are multi-dimensional, they are subjective.

Additionally, you may not experience pure forms of every emotion. You may have mixed emotions over a new job – you could feel both nervous and excited.

- The physiological response

There is a reason poets describe being in love beginning with butterflies in the stomach. You may have experienced a faster heart rate when you were afraid or a stomach lurch from anxiety. Whatever your situation, you notice that emotions cause a physiological reaction.

Many of the responses, like a racing heartbeat or sweaty palms, are regulated by the sympathetic nervous system, a part of the autonomic nervous system that deals with involuntary body responses like digestion and blood flow. It is in charge of flight or fight.

- The behavioral response

Consciously or not, you spend plenty of time looking at and assigning meaning to other people's behaviors and facial expressions. This makes the last component. The ability to interpret what someone means or how they are feeling based on their body language (facial expressions, gestures, and so forth) is tied to emotional intelligence.

Research suggests that some expressions are universal, like a smile when someone is happy, but there are cultural and social norms that affect how emotions are interpreted and expressed. In Japan, for example, people mask displays of disgust or fear in the presence of an authority figure.

Emotions versus moods

In daily communication, people use 'moods' and 'emotions' interchangeably, but according to psychologists, there are some distinctions.

An emotion is short-lived and intense. It is likely to have an identifiable cause. For instance, after a disagreement over politics, you may feel angry for a while.

On the other hand, a mood is mild but lasts longer. It is often difficult to pinpoint the cause of the mood. For example, you could feel gloomy for some days without a good reason.

Here are some short descriptions of three key emotions that you may want to learn to manage in the context of this book:

- Sadness

Sadness can be defined as a transient state characterized by grief, disinterest, disappointment, hopelessness, and a dampened mood. It is a normal emotion to experience from time to time, but sometimes people can experience it for prolonged periods like when you are depressed. It is expressed through crying, quietness, lethargy, and withdrawing from others. It could lead you to engage in coping mechanisms like avoidance and ruminating on negative thoughts, both of which stand in the way of being positive.

- Fear

Fear can play a significant role in survival. When in danger, your muscles tense, respiration and heart rate increase, and your mind is more alert to prime the body to respond appropriately. This response helps deal with threats, but if left unchecked, it can spiral out of control. Some people experience intense fear out of perceived threat or potential danger, and this is called anxiety.

- Anger

Anger can be especially powerful, characterized by feelings of agitation, hostility, frustration, and antagonism toward other people. Uncontrolled anger can cause aggressive behaviors like kicking, hitting, and hurling objects.

All emotions can have physical and mental consequences if unchecked, but this book will focus on the effects of the three and their combined emotions like embarrassment, contempt, guilt, and shame.

Why Should You Manage Emotions?

Here is an unpopular opinion: Most of the problems you have with productivity have very little to do with ideas, techniques, or tools.

Think about it, there is now, more than ever, more access to proper techniques and tools to be productive, and yet people struggle just as much.

Have you installed task management apps that have not helped with procrastination? Is it unlikely that you have emails in your inbox after you last checked two minutes ago, but you still check? Have you read books about productivity and organization, but you still waste time on unimportant things, ignoring the important tasks? What about notebooks and planners – how many do you have and how effective are they?

Are you starting to get the point?

The problem may be a bit complicated when you dig into each individual situation, but most times, it boils down to poor emotion management. Emotion management is about your reaction to strong emotions. How do you deal with sudden anxiety? What is your go-to for dealing with anger? What pops into your mind when you are criticized or ashamed?

If these questions appear difficult, it may be because you have some areas to improve when it comes to managing emotions. Think about it; from a young age, you learn how to be physically fit, how to manage finances, time management, but rarely do you learn how to manage emotions.

What you end up learning comes from emulating adults unconsciously. In other words, if your parent hit the wall when mad, you may have learned that it is okay to get physical when angry.

It is okay if your emotion management skills are unrefined, but you cannot afford to ignore working on them.

Across domains like parenting, healthcare, and investing, difficult emotions will be sure to show up. Your success in life in any area will depend on how successfully you can manage the scary emotions. It also helps with personal productivity.

As an example of how poor emotion management can get in the way of your productivity, think about procrastination. Everyone struggles with procrastination every once in a while, but it is not obvious why this happens. Imagine a day when you are trying to get a task done. You try the first time, and then the internet goes down, or you are interrupted by a phone call. You try again and find it not going as you hoped. You open your email. Before long, you decide that tomorrow is as good a day to do it as any.

Without realizing it, something psychological happened behind your procrastination. The first mistake was trying to do the task without remembering your tendencies to procrastinate, and then your mind duped you again. There are a few things to pick from this example that count as reasons to learn to manage emotions:

- Mindlessness is the enemy – If you are not vigilant when doing hard things, your emotions rule. You stand a better chance of managing the emotions when you go into the task with self-awareness.
- Your mind will resist any difficult task – This does not mean that there is a problem. It is an evolutionary heritage that the brain is always trying to save energy, so when negative self-talk begins to rear its head, you have to be aware.

Managing Emotions

To navigate through the emotional war, you have to make some major distinctions:

1. Emotions are not as easy to control – you are not a switch

Your emotions will come whether you want them or not. Once you have this settled in your mind, you can stop waiting for the emotions you do not want to go. Imagining that you can banish your emotions is not helpful and will work against you. Emotions are part of being a human being. Besides, the more you work to live according to the things you value and your commitments, the more your emotions will arise to challenge you.

2. Emotions are not negative or positive.

It is a common distinction – happiness is positive, sadness is negative, and so on. It is understandable too. The human brain cannot help but categorize things as negative or positive. It is very alert to threats.

According to modern evolutionary theory, primal emotions like fear are associated with the ancient brain parts and are suspected of having evolved among the pre-mammal ancestors. At the time, you needed to respond fast to stimuli to survive (Darwin, 1859).

Now, thanks to technology and many changes that have happened over time, life is less threatening, and you no longer need to rely on emotions in the sense of survival. Managing emotions will require you to recognize that sometimes, you will experience emotions that are not equal to the problem, and that is just alright. Rather than thinking of them as negative or positive, think of them as messengers and throw away the classifications.

3. You are not your emotions.

By their nature, emotions are intense. In the throes of an emotion like anger, you can think of yourself as an angry person. However, remind yourself that you are a human with commitments and values who happens to have some emotions triggered by certain situations. If this is your first time interacting with this idea, it may seem like it has no implications on real life, but that is not true. When you become fused to your emotions, they are in control. The alternative is observing your emotions without letting them determine how you behave.

4. You always have a choice.

A feeling or a thought on its own does not stand in the way of you acting. It is easy to make the jump from 'I am scared' to 'I can't speak', but that is the mind working at a very primal level to protect you from a perceived threat. The more authentic and accurate way is to say, 'I am scared and deciding not to speak.' The ability to observe your emotions – even the powerful ones – allows you to create space to reference your values and commitments. You do not get to choose the feelings you have, but you can choose how you respond to them. The heart of this is responsibility – which is the closest thing to a power you will ever have.

With these four distinctions forming the basis of your choices, how then can you improve your emotion management skills and get more productive?

For starters, you are bound to meet many opinions about managing emotions, and people will always have differences as a result of history, personality, struggles, culture, and so forth. Still, there are some general principles that can help you with your circumstance.

- Observe self-talk

Cognition will always go before emotion. In actuality, this looks like your productivity being derailed by negative emotion that comes as a result of subtle and powerful self-talk happening behind the scenes. Learning to observe your self-talk can help you to change your habits of thinking that you do not want and is vital in managing emotion effectively.

- Improve your vocabulary

Most people have poor emotional awareness because their vocabulary and framework for considering their emotional states is not sophisticated enough. By refining and expanding your emotional vocabulary, you can improve your self-awareness and hence your ability to manage and tolerate difficult emotions.

- Be mindful

The term mindfulness has been used a lot recently, and it could easily become cliché. However, rightly practiced and considered, it can prove vital to building your emotion management skills and improving your mental health in general. It is simply the art of keeping your attention on something you value and regulating it so that your feelings do not take hold.

- Work with a coach

There was a time you could not talk about seeing a therapist or a life coach with a straight face. There was a stigma associated with seeking help, and people assumed the worst. Nowadays, thanks to an increase in awareness, people are more open to the idea of finding help. It is much easier to find a guiding hand for a situation you find difficult. Bear in mind that an outside eye can see something that you are missing and help you in the right direction.

How Does That Connect with a Positive Outlook?

What is the use of emotional management in the context of having a positive mindset? One of the major roadblocks to being positive, as was mentioned in an earlier chapter, is emotional thinking. Being able to manage your emotions gets rid of that specific roadblock. Consider these:

- The perception of emotion

This is the ability to pinpoint emotional messages in someone's tone of voice, facial expressions, and even artistic works. People who have emotional perception of their own emotions and those of others have many advantages in social situations, and they will likely be more empathetic as they can see things from a perspective different from their own.

- Emotions to help thinking

Based on the understanding that you are not your emotions, you can rely on them to understand what you should do in a given situation. For example, if you find that you are beginning to get resentful about a situation, instead of concluding that you are generally a disagreeable person, you can alternatively unpack the situation and find out the ways that you need to grow up and how you need to speak up for yourself.

As a rule, when you are happy, you think positively, and when you are sad, you tend to have negative thoughts. When emotions are correctly used, you will first acknowledge them. From there, you ask yourself questions in a journal or when talking with a friend you trust, to help you understand the problem and to make decisions that make your life better.

- Understanding emotions

It is one thing to notice that you are feeling annoyed. However, you need to be able to know the message the emotion carries. Where is it coming from? Where can it lead you to? As an example, irritation can lead to anger or feelings of insecurity, which could cause unpredictable outbursts. Emotionally intelligent people can label their emotions appropriately and understand even complicated emotional states.

Emotional management is not getting rid of troubling emotions. It is about learning to control them. Have you ever found that when you are upset, you think that there is nothing to do? Or perhaps you try to escape to something else. Whatever the case, successful emotional management is being able to deal with whatever comes at you in a healthy and appropriate manner.

Limiting beliefs

"We all have unlimited potential — but often, our results don't reflect that. Why? Because our unconscious beliefs cripple our results. The only thing that's keeping you from getting what you want is the story you keep telling yourself."
– Tony Robbins, 1991

Sometimes, what is standing in the way of positive thinking is a limiting belief. Think back to your earliest memories as a child – do you remember being fearless? To what places did curiosity take you?

Like most people, you may notice that as you grew older, you were introduced to a long list of rules about the things you are supposed to say, how you should behave, and who you should be. Unchecked, these rules can become limiting beliefs instead of guides to help you do better in life.

To clarify, this is not a campaign to throw all the rules into the wind. Some rules exist for your benefit. However, this section is for someone who feels that they are boxed in when it comes to something they would like to do.

So what exactly is a limiting belief?

In short, a limiting belief is a mindset or belief that we make about ourselves that limits the way you think and live. It could be about you, the people you interact with, or even the world and the manner in which things run.

Here is a list of the most common limiting beliefs we tell ourselves:

- "I don't have the time."
- "It's too expensive."

- "I don't have the willpower."
- "I don't understand."
- "All the good ones are already taken."
- "I am scared of rejection."
- "I'll never find true love."
- "I don't have what it takes to succeed."
- "I don't have the talent."
- "I could never do that."
- "Successful people are just lucky."
- "Rich people are greedy."
- "I'm not good with money."
- "I'll never make enough money."
- "I can't afford that."
- "I'll never be able to retire."
- "Things will never change."

Limiting beliefs have many boundless negative effects on our lives. It could keep you from making choices that are good for you, taking advantage of new opportunities, and achieving your dreams. Ultimately, the belief keeps you stuck in a frame of mind that hinders you from living your life the way you desire.

Here are a few causes of limiting beliefs. Which one do you resonate with?

- Fear of Failure

The fear of failure is the most common fear holding us back from success. The truth is, there is no such thing as failure; there are only results. Fear destroys our mindset and immobilizes us from taking action.

- Family beliefs

Your upbringing shapes the way you think the world should look. It forms the career paths you take, the way you engage with others, and your behaviors. It is easy to develop limiting beliefs based on what you learned growing up. For example, if parents reinforce a belief that you should never challenge authority, you could become someone who does not speak up for themselves. You may believe that unfair treatment from an authority figure should be accepted. You may even be unable to recognize it.

- Education

Education plays a vital role in the limiting beliefs people adopt. Whether you are learning from friends, family, or teachers, they all impact what you accept as truth. This is because they are constantly sharing ideas, beliefs, and information on the way the world works. When you are learning from people you respect, you are more inclined to conclude whatever they tell you to be true.

- Past Experiences

When you have experiences in life, or when you make certain choices, it is common to draw conclusions based on a previous outcome. For instance, if you love someone and you get heartbroken, you could conclude that love always ends in pain. Negative experiences tend to have a shaping ability on the things you believe. It is vital to remember that your conclusions are valid only for a short time.

Identifying limiting beliefs

If limiting beliefs were easy to identify, everyone would do it, and they would be living the kind of life they want to. To recognize your limiting beliefs, you have to be willing to look within yourself and notice without judgment things that you may not even want to face. It is advisable to take a pen and paper and give yourself some time at a place you feel comfortable.

Once you have the pen and paper, do the following:

1. Identify your surface beliefs

Begin by writing down the things that you believe in general. What is it that you feel strongly about? Write also the things that influence your life every day. You can group the beliefs into different categories like relationships, career, finances, health, and family. After the exercise, examine the ones that help you to grow. Anything else may be a limiting belief.

2. Assess how you behave

Another way to know your limiting beliefs is to

examine the way you behave. Consider the times you have acted in toxic or harmful ways. Why did you do that? If you look keenly at your negative behaviors, you may find that the root cause driving your actions is a limiting belief. For example, if you have a hard time telling someone when they offend you, you may believe that conflict is bad. In turn, this could be keeping you from a truly intimate relationship.

3. Note the areas you feel challenged

If you have noticed some challenges that recur in different areas of your life, this could be because you have a limiting belief. Maybe you are unable to find a well-paid job. Or perhaps, you are unlucky in love. The challenges may be because you have adopted some untruths as truth. As you consider every challenge, write it down and note the beliefs associated with the challenge.

Overcoming limiting beliefs

Now that you have identified the beliefs that are limiting your growth, it is crucial to understand that you have the power to change. The process will not be easy, but once you commit to improvement, you will see results. To get you started, here are some tips:

- Take action toward the empowering belief

Little action equals mediocre results. The more resolved beliefs we have about achieving something, the more potential we have to accomplish it. Rather than believing, "I don't have the willpower." Start believing, "I must get it done." And take massive action towards that goal.

- Declutter

Most people are not aware that their environment can affect the things they believe. Having a spacious and well-organized environment can encourage positive thinking and improve your mental space. A tidy environment will give you space to think and gain clarity.

To do this, remove the clutter that you have accumulated over time. You can even redesign the flow and space in your home as an exercise in rearranging your psyche. The basic premise is keeping the flow of energy in your home by arranging things in a specific way.

As you do this, get rid of anything you do not like. You will notice that the exercise will influence your mind and help you to keep your thoughts on constructive things.

- Try Minimalism

Minimalism can help you to identify any false beliefs and to get rid of them. The fundamentals of the practice are honesty, detaching from material possessions, and clarity. For instance, if you are continually adding new clothing to your wardrobe, it could be that the limiting belief concerns your physical appearance. You could believe that you are not attractive if you do not have on the latest fashion. Minimalism is about resisting peer pressure and your mindset. It will help you to embrace a more meaningful lifestyle.

- Explore

Limiting beliefs and closed-mindedness are

closely related. To open your mind, let curiosity be your guide. When you give in to it, you will likely explore the world around you and get out of your comfort zone. Curiosity will create learning opportunities for you. You can start by talking with people whose backgrounds differ from yours. Traveling also helps to develop an open mind.

The world is full of beliefs and different people. This will not change. You have to find a way to adopt beliefs that support the way of life you dream of. Any idea that keeps you from that life is one to eliminate.

Conditioning empowering beliefs

Once you are ready to commit to a new empowering belief, you must condition this new belief into your subconscious. Here are some ways you can do this:

- Practice visualization

Visualization has been used for ages by successful people to picture their desired outcomes. It gives you what appears to the onlooker like superpowers, helping you to create your dream life by accomplishing one task or goal at a time. Elite athletes use visualization to focus on their goals. It activates the subconscious, which generates creative ideas to achieve that goal. It programs the brain to recognize and see resources needed in the service of the goal, it activates the law of attraction, and it helps to build your internal motivation to do what you need to do to achieve your dreams.

Visualization is simple - Sit in a comfortable place and close your eyes. Imagine in as much detail as you can. Imagine looking out through your eyes when you have reached the ideal. Do this a few minutes every day. The best time is after you wake up and right before going to bed. Follow the following steps:

1. Imagine sitting in a theater. Dim the lights and have the movie start. The movie is of your life and the changes that happen when you have embraced the new belief. Picture as many details as you can, including what you are wearing, your body movements, and the expressions on your face. Recreate in your body the feelings you would associate with the activity.

2. Leave your chair and move to the screen. Enter into the movie and experience it again inside of yourself. This is referred to as the 'embodied

image' instead of the 'distant image.' It will deepen your experience.

3. Walk back out of the screen and return to your seat. Grab the screen and shrink it to the size of a cracker. Put the tiny screen into your mouth and swallow. Imagine each piece like a hologram containing the picture of the successful you. Think of the screens moving through your bloodstream into every cell in your body.

- Anchoring

An anchor holds your attention to help you focus on the desirable belief you want to hold instead of drifting away. In the process of anchoring, you associate an internal response with a trigger outside so that the belief can be re-accessed quickly. A psychological anchor will act as a reference point to stabilize the mental state you want.

There are factors that will contribute to the power of an anchor, including the intensity and richness of the experience, its emotional level, and the continuous reinforcement of the anchor. The idea is simple; when two events happen close together enough times, they become associated with each other. Use the following steps:

1. Think of the belief you want to adopt. Think back to a time when you embodied it, like when you won a prize or received some good news or even your first kiss.
2. Tell the story of what happened in your head and the events that lead to that moment. Describe them as vividly as you can until you remember the feeling.

3. Hold your middle and left index fingers in your right hand and squeeze gently. As you squeeze another time, make the picture in your head last longer.
4. Describe the feeling again and your thoughts at the time while squeezing the fingers the same way.

You can repeat this process for as many times as you like until the action triggers the thoughts and feelings immediately. You can make the action anything you want.

- Emotional Freedom Technique (EFT)

EFT can help you when you are in emotional distress because of a limiting belief. The technique is founded on research that found that a disruption in energy causes pain and negative emotions. The technique is about balancing your energy system.

There are energy spots in the body that you can tap to restore its energy and relieve the symptoms of a negative experience. You can use the following steps to address different issues:

1. Find the issue -This technique will only be effective if you know what belief you want to address. It will be your focal point as you tap. Focus on only one belief at a time.
2. Test its initial intensity – After finding the problem, benchmark its intensity and rate anywhere between 0 and 10. 10 is the most difficult. The scale is an assessment of the discomfort you feel from the main issue. A benchmark helps to monitor progress.

3. The set up – Establish a phrase explaining the belief you want to change. You want to focus on acknowledging the issue and self-acceptance. A set up could sound like: 'Even if I have (this problem), I completely accept myself.' You can change the phrase to fit your issue.

4. The tapping sequence – EFT tapping sequence addresses nine meridian points. There are 12 major points mirroring each side of the body and corresponding to an organ. Still, EFT focuses on the small intestine meridian (karate chop), the governing vessel (top of the head), bladder meridian (eyebrow), gallbladder meridian (side of the eye), stomach meridian (under the eye), governing vessel (under the nose), the central vessel (chin), kidney (beginning

of the collarbone), and spleen meridian (under the arm). Start by tapping the karate chop as you recite your set-up phrase thrice. Tap the rest of the points in the order they are listed. Finish the sequence at the top of the head point. Be sure to keep you focus on the problem area as you recite the setup phrase and repeat the sequence up to three times.

5. Testing the intensity – After the sequence, use the scale of 0 to 10 and compare the intensity levels. Repeat until you reach an intensity level of zero.

- Emulating people who actively live the empowering belief

You can be the best person at something in the world, but if you do not present yourself that way, you will not feel confident. One way to overcome a limiting belief and translate that feeling of inner confidence is to find someone to emulate.

Do you know someone who lives out the empowering belief? That's an excellent start. Now assume that you are an understudy and watch what they do, their mannerisms, what they say, and how they present themselves to people. Practice doing the same things. As a rule of thumb, find someone who does not intimidate you.

When you emulate someone, you set yourself free from your identity. It does not matter how unconfident, introverted, or clumsy you feel. If you walk into a room and assume the belief you want, you will begin to feel it. Over time, it will come naturally to you and carry you through other situations.

Summary

Emotions are a big part of having a positive mindset. They inform the decisions you make. You can use them as a friend, or you can leave them, and they would work against you. The basis of emotional management is understanding that:

- You are not your emotions
- Emotions are neither positive nor negative; acknowledging them without labels is best
- You always have a choice when it comes to responding
- You cannot switch off emotions or switch them on – you have to learn to negotiate with yourself

With these factors as the basis for your emotion management, you can work to counter mindlessness and adopt the suggested methods including:

- Watching your self-talk
- Improving your vocabulary
- Being mindful
- Enlisting the help of a coach if you need it.

This chapter also looks into limiting beliefs and helps you to identify and overcome them using neurolinguistic programming techniques like anchoring, EFT, and visualization.

Positive Mindset Mastery

Chapter 5: Managing Your Relationships

People define relationships differently, but most agree that for a relationship to be healthy, there has to be some components like honesty, openness, and safe communication. For any kind of relationship, you have to be sure you understand each other's expectations and needs so that you are on the same page. You cannot be on the same page if you do not talk to each other.

As a rule of thumb, if something is bothering

you in a relationship, you have to be willing to talk about it rather than keep it in. Each person in the relationship bears the responsibility to make themselves a safe place for the other. One way to do this is to respect the feelings and wishes of the other person. You want to let them know that you are putting an effort to think about their ideas as you make choices.

Compromise is also an essential feature of relationships. Even healthy relationships have disagreements, but you have to figure out a way to solve conflicts rationally and fairly when they happen.

A healthy relationship is not based on control and power; it is based on respect and equality.

It is important to remember that you cannot have relationships if you are unwilling to be who you truly are in front of your friends or partner. Yet, there is a measure of wisdom in controlling who you let into your personal space. They could influence the way you think and get in the way or support whatever dreams and ambitions you may have.

Good Relationships? Why?

Human beings are, by nature, social beings – you crave positive interactions and friendships the way you crave water and food. It makes sense that the better your relationships, the more productive, happy, and positive you will be.

Good relationships at work, for example, make the environment more enjoyable. People will be more likely to comply if there are any changes to implement if they have good relationships. It also helps with creativity and innovation.

Good relationships anywhere will give you freedom. Rather than spend your energy and time overcoming the problems of negative relationships, you can focus on the opportunities that come your way. They help to develop careers. Imagine a boss who does not trust you – how likely are they to promote you when it is time?

It is often said that the 'ship' in the term relationship is a reference to the fact that the relationship either sinks or floats. While that is not entirely true, it is useful to think about the relationships in that perspective and consider which ones are worth keeping.

What Makes a Good Relationship?

Here are the keys to a healthy relationship:

- Trust – This forms the basis of every relationship. When you trust a colleague, teammate, or friend, you develop a powerful bond that will help with effective communication. You tell them your thoughts openly, your actions are easy to understand, and people do not have to waste their time 'watching their back' with you.
- Mutual respect – when you respect someone, you value their ideas and input as they do yours. You work together to come up with solutions based on your collective creativity, insight, and wisdom.
- Mindfulness – This is taking responsibility for your actions and words. Mindful

people are careful about what they say. They will not let their negative emotions affect their friends.

- Embracing diversity – Good relationships not only accept diversity in people, but they also embrace diverse opinions and even welcome them. For example, when your colleagues and friends offer a view that is different from yours, you consider what they say and factor their insights into your decision.

- Open communication – People are always communicating through messages, emails, and face to face. The more effectively you communicate, the richer the relationships will be. Every good relationship depends on honest and open communication.

Relationships at Work

It makes sense to try and maintain good working relationships with all people, but some relationships deserve more attention.

For instance, you will benefit from a good relationship with major stakeholders in your company, as those are people who have a say in your failure or success. Forming a bond with them helps you to make sure your career and projects are on track.

Tips for building good work relationships

You spend a lot of your life at work, so it makes sense that you would want to build better relationships. You do not want the environment you go to every day to be what stands in the way of a positive outlook in life.

- Develop people skills

Good relationships begin with well-developed people skills. How are your soft skills? How well do you communicate, collaborate, and handle conflict?

- Know your relationship needs

What is it that you need from others? What do they need from you? Understanding needs can be crucial to having better relationships.

- Schedule time to make better relationships

Devote a chunk of your day, even if it is simply 20 minutes spread throughout the day, toward building relationships. You could check up on someone at lunchtime, reply to their LinkedIn or Twitter, or ask someone to a cup of coffee. The little interactions create the basis for a good relationship.

- Build your emotional intelligence

If you are going to have good relationships, you need to spend some time developing how well you recognize your own emotions and understanding the message they portray. The more you improve your emotional intelligence, the better you will be able to understand the needs and emotions of others.

- Say "Thank You"

When someone helps you, be keen to show appreciation. Everyone from your office cleaner to your boss wants to be appreciated for what they do. Compliment people genuinely, and that will open the doors to closer relationships.

- Manage your boundaries

Be sure to manage and set boundaries appropriately. Boundaries help you to interact with people in a way that you feel respected. They help you to have an impact without feeling taken advantage of. If you notice that a colleague or a friend has a monopoly on your time, you may need to assert your boundaries so that you can have time to work and time for social interactions.

- Do not gossip

Office politics can kill relationships at work. If you have a conflict with someone within your group, address it with them. If you gossip about the situation, you will only make it worse and create animosity and mistrust.

- Listen actively

When talking to colleagues and customers, practice active listening. People respond well when others genuinely hear what they have to say. Listen more than you speak, and you will be someone that people can trust.

Ten Tips to Keep Any Relationship Healthy

Other than your work relationships, you have to care for your relationship with your significant other, friends outside of work, and family members. It is easy to make things more complicated than they should be, so follow the following basic rules to begin moving in the right direction:

1. Good relationships take work

Remember that movie when the girl met a boy and they were married in 90 minutes? Well, that is only true in movies. Good relationships do not happen in a vacuum. The parties involved have to risk sharing what is happening in their heads and hearts.

2. You can only change yourself; you cannot change anyone else

If you love a person and think that they will change the way they behave to get rid of things you are uncomfortable with, you need to re-think your strategy. If you want anything to change, discuss with your partner so that they know what you need, but remember that you can only change yourself.

3. All arguments come from pain or fear

When you are upset or hurt, find out what is happening in the other person's mind instead of getting angry with them. You will find that people are not usually upset for the reasons you think.

4. Understand gender differences

Men may not be from Mars and women from Venus, but the differences between the genders are inevitable and part of biology. You can either learn to celebrate and understand them or make other people's lives miserable, trying to mold them into your own image.

5. Honor each other every day

There is a popular saying that every day is a second chance. Take as many opportunities as you need to make your relationship deeper and gratifying. Feeling cherished and respected by someone you love makes life easier.

6. Anger wastes time

Anger kills relationships because it is self-absorbed and blinding. When you are annoyed with someone, allow yourself time to keep calm, and then gently discuss what is happening in your mind.

7. Regular tune-ups are a necessity

It is okay to read a book on relationships, even when everything is going well. You may pick up some ideas that could strengthen the connection you have.

8. Find ways to stay close

This is more important in romantic relationships but cuts across every type of relationship. Find creative ways to devote more time together.

9. Take responsibility for your happiness

No person can give you happiness. It is something you have to give yourself. If you start to feel that someone else is the reason you are unhappy, look inside and identify what you are missing.

10. Give what you would like to get

People's needs are ever-changing. If you want to be understood, try to be understanding. If you want to feel love, try giving it more. This is a simple rule, but it works. You want to be proactive in your relationships.

Difficult Relationships

You want all your relationships to go well, but occasionally, you will have to collaborate with people you would rather not work with or people you cannot relate to. For the sake of work, for example, you have to keep the relationship professional.

When this is the case, you want to make an effort to know that person. They likely know you are not on good terms, so you may want to make the first move to work on the relationship. As a rule of thumb, make sure that your conversation is genuine. Try not to be so guarded that it is impossible to get close. Ask about their interests, background, and successes in the past. Remember not to focus on your differences, but try to find the things you have in common.

Keep in mind that not all relationships will be great, but they could at least be workable.

When you have done everything you can, and it

still does not work, it may be time to end the relationship.

Tips for Ending a Bad Relationship

Moving on is not always easy. You may have difficulties convincing yourself that that is the right thing to do.

As a way of assurance, if a relationship makes you more miserable than happy and your heart is not right, you do not have to hold on to the relationship. It may not mean that you are wrong or that they are, just that you are not right for each other. If you feel stuck, the following are research-based psychological strategies to help you make that difficult decision:

- Separate love and addiction

Neurochemically speaking, love and addiction are similar. Studies show that when partners are intensely in love and they see images of their beloved, the brain region that is activated is the same region that gets activated in drug addicts when they crave a fix. However, even though love has some qualities that look like addiction, healthy love should also have other attributes like trust, commitment, and respect. These are qualities that will keep the relationship strong even when the passion and excitement are not at the top.

Addictive love is focused on getting to the 'highs' whatever the cost. The people involved have unpredictable behaviors – like not calling when they promise to. They will likely keep you hooked because their inconsistent affection always leaves you wanting more.

While trying to get out of any relationship that feels more like an addiction than a loving bond, you will need to reframe your emotions and thoughts about the person. This may require you to get some healthy distance – you can go for a while without calling until the longing reduces. When you are overwhelmed, acknowledge the feeling but do not act on it.

- Take a break

Your family and friends can be divided into two categories:

I. The ones who make you feel good, who always reassure you, and with whom you are confident that everything will work.

II. The ones who continuously drain your energy with subtle and blatant implications that you are weak, silly, or pathetic.

If you find yourself drawn to both, you want comfort, but you also need the motivation to change. One way to achieve this without berating or deluding yourself is to practice self-compassion. Self-compassion involves reassuring yourself that you are not a horrible person and that it is understandable to love someone you would prefer not to. Many people get into this kind of situation. Self-compassion is about caring for yourself and seeking your best interests. It involves you re-parenting yourself, which may mean leaving a relationship that keeps hurting you.

- Create a plan

Research has proven that you are more likely to

make lasting changes when you create specific goals rather than 'if/then' plans. When you have a specific plan, you can break it down into simple steps that you can do every day. That way, you do not have to wonder about the way forward, and you are more gracious when relating to others.

It is possible that when leaving a relationship, you have many if/then connections. On examination, you will find that they do not work in your favor. An example is thinking: "If I am lonely and missing my partner, I will call them and invite them over." Instead, take up a habit that will make you a better person in the long run, like listening to empowering messages or reading. The more you make different choices, the more you get rid of the 'if' stimulus and the automatic links attached. You will make it easier to resist the old patterns.

- Fight cognitive dissonance

Your mind has sneaky ways of justifying your actions so that you do not feel like you made a mistake or did a stupid thing. This is called cognitive dissonance. It is the reason you find yourself loyal to a group that caused you suffering. It is also why bad relationships are difficult to break free from, especially when you have been in the relationship for an extended period.

Unless things in the relationship went awry suddenly, ending a relationship often means reconciling with the fact that you did not end it when you could have, and that was a mistake you made. If you are unable to reconcile with this, you might keep rationalizing your commitment to the relationship to justify the past decision to stay in it. It helps to be aware of the tricks of the mind to avoid the trap.

- Own your decision

Ending a relationship can be a painful and prolonged struggle that is difficult to do alone. You may need to get the support of someone else to help you keep the course and to fill your life with positive and healthy activities. Ultimately though, the choice to end it has to be yours. Succumbing to outside pressure will not last you long. When other things fail, it helps to ask yourself what you really want and accept the answer.

Summary

In this chapter, you have learned how integral relationships are to your mindset. If you are constantly interacting with people who put you on the defense or people who are toxic for you, it will be harder to stay positive.

You have learned how to foster healthy relationships by growing your people skills, scheduling time for relationships you care about, establishing and maintaining boundaries, knowing your needs, and seeking to meet them.

Healthy relationships:

- Take work
- Require you to change yourself, not the other person
- Need regular tune-ups
- Need a proper understanding of arguments and where they stem from
- Rely on ways people put in place to stay close
- Require that parties take responsibility for their happiness

- Need reciprocity
- Need healthy ways to deal with anger
- Require honor

Unfortunately, not all relationships you will be in will be healthy or have people working to make them better. When you encounter difficult relationships, you have to be equipped to end them by:

- Separating love and addiction
- Fighting cognitive dissonance
- Taking a break when you need it
- Creating a plan
- Owning your choice to end the relationship

Positive Mindset Mastery

Chapter 6: Neuro-Linguistic Programming

Neuro-linguistic programming (NLP) is like a user manual for your brain. The previous chapter concentrated on your external environment. While that is significant to the way you live and think, the ultimate battle has to be won in your brain, and NLP can help with that.

Beginning the 1970s, researchers found out that NLP techniques can be effective in changing the way you experience the world. Since your feelings and thoughts shape your reality, this means that using techniques that alter those thoughts and feelings can change the trajectory of your life.

NLP is about offering practical ways to change the way you think. It changes how you interact with the events in your past and ultimately affects your approach to life. The techniques discussed in this chapter will show you how to control your life by controlling your mind. Where psychotherapy focuses on the 'why', NLP focuses on the 'how' and gives you practical guidelines.

It was co-created by psychotherapists Richard Bandler and Virginia Satir. Bandler noticed that the conventional techniques used in psychotherapy did not always work. He was concerned with finding different ways to solve problems. NLP was born as a result of techniques that worked well with their patients.

The principle behind NLP is taking control of one's mind. You may not have much control over what is happening around you, but you can control the thoughts you have about it. This stems from an understanding that your thoughts, emotions, and feelings are not things that you have or things that define you; they are choices that you make. You choose to think a particular way. The root causes may be complicated and could range from the comments of people, to beliefs from your teachers, parents, or even events you went through.

NLP will show you how to control your influences and beliefs. Using mind techniques like reframing content can change how you feel and think about events of the past, phobias, and fears from the perspective that while you cannot control what happens, you can control how you handle it.

NLP is inherently connected with the power of belief. If you are convinced that something bad will happen, no matter the evidence to the contrary, your brain will only focus on the negative, and something bad will inevitably happen. On the converse, if you believe that something will make you better, you will often become better – like with medical experiments and the placebo effect.

The bottom line here is that whatever you believe yourself capable of achieving is possible for you. However, you have to challenge your limiting beliefs. Ask questions like – How can I be sure I can do that? When did I first think I cannot? How was that wrong?

The other pillar of NLP is setting goals. There are universally known principles of setting goals, but NLP suggests some additional insights focusing less on dissatisfaction and more on satisfaction.

For instance, your goals must be positive so that you focus on the things you want and not the things you lose in your efforts to get what you want. You are to think about the things you truly want – for example, it is not the purchase of a dream house that drives you, but the hope of living in it. It is easier to stay motivated about a goal that gives you satisfaction.

NLP believes in the power of questions and their ability to help with clarity. According to Bandler, the mind is set up to look for answers to questions actively. If you ask yourself a question like 'why am I feeling so bad?', your mind will come up with many answers, and you will likely feel worse. When using NLP, it is not just about asking questions but asking the right questions like – why do I want to change? What do I need to focus on to improve? What will life look like after I have changed?

NLP uses questions whose natural result is a positive outlook. Here are a few tools used in NLP:

- Moving images

Bring the image of a person who aggravates you to mind. What does the picture look like in your mind? Zoom the image out, change it to black and white, and then imagine the image fading away. How does that make you feel?

Now imagine the picture of something that evokes positive feelings in you. Zoom it in and make it brighter and more prominent. As it moves closer to you, how does it make you feel?

The idea of moving images is about allowing this thought process to help you to recognize the effect of events and people and to understand what you feel about them. By playing around with the images, you teach your brain how to focus on the good feelings and to ignore the bad feelings.

- Diminishing the inner voice

Most people will admit to having an inner critical voice in their heads that shows up at the worst of times. It says things like 'that sounds so hard for a person like you,' or 'you are not able to do that.' The next time that critical voice speaks up imagine that it sounds like Tweety Bird or Donald Duck. How do the changes make you feel about the wisdom of that voice? If the voice does not sound real, it will be easier to silence.

- Playing a movie backward

If you just went through a difficult experience and you are having a hard time processing it, imagine if it happened backward. Begin from the point when you realized that it was finally over. Now imagine the incident unfolding backward until you get to a time before it starts. Do this several times until you know how the film unfolds in reverse. Now make it small in your mind - maybe so little that you can only see it on your phone –and play it backward. Eventually, think of a different end to that experience as long as it makes you smile. Do you feel the change in your emotions? The principal technique is that your brain learns another way to think of a memory to change the way you respond to it.

- Brilliance squared

Consider an emotion that you are interested in feeling, like confidence. Imagine that there is a colored square before you and the color of it is the one you associate with the emotion. Now imagine you are standing on the square and it is full of that emotion. How would you stand? What would be the look in your face? What about your posture? Step inside the square and behave like the imaginary you. What feeling spreads through you? Keep repeating until the process comes easy. Now imagine the square before you and enter. What does it feel like?

The trick here is to train your mind to make associations of a feeling and an image. When you conjure the image, you will conjure the feeling.

Hopefully, these examples have demonstrated NLP to be a powerful tool based on the power of your mind. Some people may think of them as mind tricks, but relying on these tried techniques teaches you how to control your mind and your responses to it.

Here are five techniques to use on your journey to becoming a more positive person:

Dissociation

Have you ever found yourself in a situation that evokes a bad feeling in you? Perhaps it is an experience that reminded you of a previous experience, or maybe it is something that makes you feel down each time you encounter it. Do you get nervous when a specific person approaches you? – a crush, perhaps? These feelings of nervousness, sadness, or shyness can appear to be unstoppable or automatic, but the NLP technique of dissociation can help you.

Identify the emotion that you feel – is it discomfort, rage, fear, or dislike for the situation? Do you want to get rid of it? Now imagine that you had the ability to float outside your body and see yourself from outside – the idea is to give you an observer's perspective. Do you notice the change in your feelings?

If you want to get an extra boost, you can imagine floating outside of your body, looking at yourself, and then getting back into your body again to look at yourself while you are looking at yourself. The double dissociation will get rid of the negative emotion or at least make it so minor that you can deal with it.

There are guided audios that you can use to help you with this technique, and most of them use imagery and hypnotic language as well to help you to handle overwhelming feelings like phobias, anger, fear, sadness, grief, and jealousy.

In essence, three things are critical to making an enduring change:

- You have to be tired enough of dealing with the same problem over and over until that drives change
- You have to change the perspective through which you see the problem so that you see it in a new light

- You have to come up with an appealing option that will be worthy enough for you to pursue

The simplest way to go about it is to change your perspective. There is a common expression that 'you can't see the forest for the trees' used to describe someone who is too involved in the details of a problem to see the situation as a whole. When you are in the moment, it is easy to be too close that you see nothing else but the trees. Back up and view yourself as you have the experience. That way, you dissociate from it.

You allow your mind to give you another viewpoint. You are an observer. This is a powerful technique that you can use any time you like. You have to be careful, though, that you do not shove emotions into the shadow.

The point is not to become emotionless but to process the emotions and to introduce options.

Dissociation helps to deal with the delusion that you are your sadness or that you are your anger. When you are stuck in the feelings, and you become the feeling, it will be difficult for it to ever change – the process is called nominalizing, and it is one of the biggest problems that people face.

The dissociation technique helps you to see 'the forest even as you are facing the trees' and to set yourself free of overwhelming emotions. However, it takes courage to do this technique and do it well. For a moment, it will cause you to experience deep feelings which many people are afraid of, but it will help you if you take the time to do that. Before you begin, think of a negative experience or feeling that is persistent that you would like to change forever.

Content Reframing

Try content reframing when you start to feel that a situation is helpless and negative. Reframing will remove the negativity in the situation and will empower you by changing the meaning that you assign to the experience into something positive.

For instance, say a relationship you care about has just ended. This on the surface may seem awful, but there are ways to reframe it so that it is bearable. Ask questions like: Are there benefits to being single? You now have many options when it comes to potential relationships. You also get the freedom to do the things you want when you feel like doing them. You can even think about the lessons you have learned from the relationship that would help you to have better relationships in the days to come.

In circumstances that you were expecting something bad to happen, it is easy to feel afraid and to focus on that fear, but that only causes more problems. You can instead focus on the responsibility you have to yourself. That way, you empower yourself to get out of the situation.

Essentially, content reframing is about assigning a different meaning by re-examining past experiences. It is going back to an event in your mind and finding alternative explanations to events that you find disturbing. It helps you to implement new desired behaviors or to get over hurtful words that were said about you.

It is vital to note that reframing in life happens

regardless of NLP. Conscious or not, your brain will create meaning and assign them to different events. Context framing is about choosing to assign a meaning that works for your betterment.

A frame offers a context or a focus for your actions and thoughts. The way the frame in a picture puts boundaries and borders on what you see in the picture, a frame of reference helps you live out your beliefs and to know how to interact with others and with yourself. It lets you see what your perceived role in life is and your perceived skills, abilities, and limitations. People are constantly setting frames, limits, and boundaries on the things you can do and those you cannot do, and they sometimes do this without thinking about the truthfulness of the limitations and their consequences.

Changing the frame when you have had an experience can influence a lot the way that you perceive, react, and interpret the experience. If you are told that you have just one hour to finish a task, that will cause you to be anxious and may stand in the way of doing that task well, affecting the quality as opposed to if you had a whole week to complete the same task. This is an illustration of how one detail in the frame can impact the choices that you make.

Reframing is about improving your experience and hence improving your actions to see the impact of your beliefs. It is more resourceful than any choice that you may make in your reaction.

When trying to reframe content, ask yourself questions such as: What other meaning could this event have? In what ways could this prove to be a resource or a positive experience?

When you reframe the content or the meaning of an event, you are choosing the specific aspects that you will focus on. You can, for example, see an electrical power failure as a disruptive occurrence and a disaster given everything you have to do, or you can see it as an opportunity for you to spend quality time with your loved ones and to have fun in innovative ways.

You can use content reframing for statements like, 'I get angry when my boss hovers as I work.' Do you see how the persona has taken an event and assigned meaning to it? Granted, the association could be true; it also limits how resourceful the person is and what they can do in such instances. To reframe the situation, think about the underlying assumption of NLP that 'each behavior action has a positive intent.'

Ask yourself questions like: What is your boss looking to achieve with this behavior? Why does he do it? Is there a positive value in his actions? The positive value could be on the side of the boss or the employee in this case. You could reframe the situation like: 'it is a good thing that you know your boundaries well enough and are unwilling to let people violate them.'

Content reframing is about finding the lessons in every experience and finding meaning in life.

Anchoring Yourself

Anchoring came from a Russian scientist, Ivan Pavlov, who experimented with dogs. He rang a bell repeatedly every time the dogs were eating. After repeating the experiment for a while, he could ring the bell and have the dogs drooling regardless of the time, even if there was no food available.

The action created an association between the behavior of eating and the bell – conditioned response.

With this NLP technique, you can use stimulus-response anchors to form habits.

Anchoring will help you to form associations between a positive emotional response that you desire and a specific sensation or phrase. When you pick a positive thought or emotion and connect it deliberately to a gesture, you can make it an anchor to use anytime you feel low to change your feelings immediately.

To anchor yourself, identify a feeling you want

to experience, whether it be calmness, confidence, or happiness. Find a place on your body where you would like to anchor the emotion. It could be with a simple action like squeezing a fingernail, pulling an earlobe, or touching a knuckle. It does not matter where you pick, just as long it is a place that is unique enough that you are not constantly touching it.

Think back to a time in the past when you felt the state that you want. Go back to that time mentally and float into your body. Look through your eyes and relive the memory. Be careful to adjust your body language so that it matches that state and memory. Tour through the things you saw, listen for thing things you heard, and feel what you remember feeling. You will start to enter into that state. This step compares to recounting a funny story from the past to your friend and as you get into it more, you laugh again because of the associations to the story that allow you to relive it.

As you inhabit the memory, squeeze, touch, or pull the body area that you chose. As you relive the memory, your brain will make associations between the memory and the gesture. Release the touch when the emotional peak begins to wear off. This will form a stimulus-response that will trigger the state every time you make that touch. To feel it, you just have to touch yourself that same way.

If you want to strengthen the response, you can think of another memory where you felt the same state. Return and relive it through your eyes. Anchor it on the same spot. Whenever you add a memory, the anchor gains potency, and the response it will trigger will be stronger. You can use this technique whenever you want to change your mood.

Anchoring is fundamental in NLP and can help you feel more enthusiastic, confident, and relaxed as you meet new people.

It is an easy way to let you change unwanted feelings to resourceful feelings in moments. When you create an anchor, you create a stimulus-response pattern to allow you to feel however you want, whenever you want.

In essence, you associate an internal response to an external trigger so that it can happen fast and often covertly. The association is considered reflexive, and not something you choose.

In NLP, anchoring has been expanded to include some connections between other experiential aspects beyond the behavioral responses and environmental cues. A remembered photo, for example, could become an anchor for a specific feeling. A tone of voice could also become an anchor for a state of confidence or excitement. A person could consciously decide to create and re-trigger the associations instead of them being a mindless and knee-jerk reflex. That way, you use an anchor as a tool for self-empowerment. Anchoring can help to establish and reactivate mental processes associated with learning, creativity, and concentration.

Rapport

The dictionary definition of rapport is a relationship marked by conformity, affinity, and harmony. It supports alignment, agreement, and similarity.

NLP rapport is the ability to relate to others or

make them feel like you do in a way that will create understanding and trust. It is the ability to see beyond your perspective into the other person's and to have them understand yours. You do not have to agree with the perspective they have, and you do not have to like it. This technique makes any communication easy.

There are many ways to build rapport, but one of the fastest and most effective ways comes from NLP. In this technique, you subtly mirror the other person's body language, words, and tone of voice.

People are drawn to others who are like them. By mirroring the other person subtly, their brain will fire off mirror neurons and pleasure sensors to make them like you.

This technique is easy; sit or stand the way a

person is standing and tilt your head the way that they have. When they smile, smile as well, and mirror their facial expression. When they cross their legs, cross yours and imitate their voice.

You have to be subtle when trying to create rapport. If you do the activities overtly, the other person will consciously notice, and that breaks rapport, so be sure to mirror calmly and naturally.

A successful interaction hugely depends on people's ability to establish and keep rapport. In fact, more business decisions are made based on rapport than technical merit of the business. You will likely make purchases from people you agree with and offer support to a person that you can relate with than someone you find it hard to understand.

NLP rapport techniques are powerful in their effects and implications. There are two ways that you can learn to view other people. You can choose to emphasize what you have that is not common, or you can zoom in on the similarities. You can always figure out a thing or two that you share with a person, even if it is your humanity. In the same way, you will always have differences with other people.

When you zero in on the differences, establishing rapport becomes difficult. By dwelling on the things that you have in common, antagonism and resistance disappear, and cooperation improves. The good news is that as you practice, it becomes easier to identify the things you have in common with others and to focus on those.

A significant feature of NLP rapport is pacing.

Pacing is what maintains that rapport. By definition, it is the process of moving the way the other person moves. In doing so, you accept their behavior and set them up as a model for existing in the world. Rapport is concerned with reducing the perceived or real differences at an unconscious level.

You can pace different aspects of behavior, as you saw in the examples given earlier. Note that if the other person catches on to what you are doing, it can become awkward – any obvious attempts of imitating will break the harmony. Pacing has to be unconscious. After rapport has been established, you can influence the behavior of the other person. One way to confirm rapport is that when you make a movement, the other person follows you. For example, if you scratch your nose or yawn, they will do the same.

Matching happens naturally in some contexts. Watch someone as they have a conversation with a small child. They will likely crouch to get to the height of the child and will talk excitedly or slowly based on the situation. In restaurants, romantic couples often appear engaged in some sort of dance as they lean and smile at each other in mirroring postures.

To create rapport, you can also adjust your whole body, a part of it, or half of it to match the other person. You can match the poses they offer with their shoulders or head. However, if the body posture is unusual, do not match it, or it will seem disrespectful. You have to be subtle.

You can also match other aspects like voice and breathing. You can match the rate of a person's breathing or the depth of it, just as long as you do not do it to a person with difficulty breathing.

As for the voice, match the pitch, volume, pace, type of words, and tone. This may be difficult to learn, but it will be worth it when you do. You do not have to match everything; you can just choose one. If a person speaks slowly, slow your speech down as well. If they speak softly, drop the volume in your voice.

You can create rapport by authentically trying to understand another person's values and beliefs without judging them. It is important to remember that the goal is not to change their values, agree with them, or even dispute; it is to understand.

The final aspect that you can match is the language pattern. Many people in the marketing and sales sectors match language patterns. Here, you use the same words to describe processes and things so that the person feels understood.

Persuasion and Influence

A lot of the work in NLP is dedicated to helping people get rid of their negative emotions, bad habits, and limiting beliefs. Influence and persuasion are about changing the way people do or perceive things ethically. They help you to deal with the contribution of relationships to a positive mindset as earlier discussed and can be thought of as a way to manage relationships.

One of the major contributors to the field, Milton Erickson, was a psychiatrist who studied the subconscious mind and used hypnotherapy to understand it. He had mastered hypnosis to the point that he found a way to communicate with the subconscious minds of other people outside of hypnosis. It is said that he could hypnotize people anywhere and anytime in normal conversations. His methods of hypnosis were later developed to be called conversational hypnosis.

Conversational hypnosis can be used to persuade and influence people and to help them to get over their fears, conflict, and limiting beliefs. It is useful for reaching people who are resistant.

Use the following tips to influence and persuade people:

- Framing – This is a technique that is common in politics. A common example is the inheritance tax. Politicians fighting the tax call it the 'death tax'. The term 'death' instead of 'inheritance' causes people to make negative associations with it. Framing is not obtrusive, but using emotive words can convince people to accept your perspective.

- Reflection – Reflecting is imitating the movements someone makes. It happens unconsciously, but you can do it intentionally. Try to be imperceptible and reflect them at intervals of two to four seconds between movements.

- Deficit – This technique is common with advertisers. Opportunities are more attractive if they have limited access or limited time offers. For example, free shipping, discount code, or a free gift that's available for a limited time only. This method works if you use it appropriately, but you have to stay on your guard. Think about how the technique will affect you as well.

- Interchange – When someone does something nice for you, you feel compelled to reciprocate. The idea here is to do something nice for people you would like something from. No matter who it is, be sure to take the initiative first.
- Timing – People are usually more flexible and docile when they are tired. Before asking something of someone, you can bide time until they have exerted considerable mental effort. Catching a colleague at the end of the day could mean that no matter what you ask, they will promise to do it the next day.
- Congruence – Everyone is subconsciously trying to be consistent. An example of this technique is with

sellers. A seller will likely shake hands as you negotiate a purchase. Most people make associations of that with the completion of a deal. Shaking hands before a sale is complete increases the chances that you will agree with the seller. You can use this technique to persuade people to do something before their logical mind comes alive.

- Smooth speech – In normal conversation, people will use phrases and exclamations to express uncertainty, like 'hmm' or 'well'. These words make you sound less convincing. Try to speak without them, and you will sound more confident and persuasive.
- Authorities and friends – You are likely to convince others to follow things that

are important to you if you consider an authority.

Summary

NLP techniques are a user manual for the brain. They are tools to help you to take control of your thoughts and your feelings. They work by begging questions whose natural answer is a positive outlook.

From this chapter, you have learned how to use:

- Dissociation – the ability to step away from a situation so that you see the big picture and then align yourself properly
- Content framing – grabbing the lesson in a situation by shifting the perspective
- Anchoring – associating an action with a feeling or thought so that you can access it with a simple step when you need it

- Rapport – relating to other people in ways that reduce the visible differences between you
- Persuasion and influence – using techniques to ethically convince people to adopt a different mode of being or doing things

Chapter 7: Daily Rituals for a Positive Mindset

Why Rituals are Important

Your future is not shaped by the major events or decisions in your life but by your daily habits. What you do every day; the choices you make define who you become. That is the place of rituals. They give you a sense of control.

In this chapter, rituals are not religious ceremonies or obsessive-compulsive habits; they are practical things you do every day. Imagine going for a first date or a job interview; do you feel anxious? When the situation ahead of you is uncertain, rituals help you to focus. They increase your performance by making small mundane acts significant and bringing with them joy and meaning.

When you are looking to change your mindset, nothing you do will work if you do not pour your heart into it. Rituals are symbolic acts that will help you engage your emotions. According to Bronislaw Malinowski, you turn to rituals when the outcome you want is important, outside of your control and uncertain.

The point is that even if rituals are associated with maintaining the status quo, the repetition has a significant effect beyond appearing a certain way to others. Rituals have been used in many cultures to deal with grief or increase confidence and reduce anxiety. They do not need to be communal. In the case of changing your mindset, rituals will likely be private and personal.

Rituals will shape how you perceive yourself. They will boost your self-confidence by improving focus and execution. This is the reason professional athletes, for example, will have a set of activities they perform before a competition.

When things are challenging, rituals can help to kill procrastination. They lower your anxiety levels and help you start a project you would otherwise leave untouched. They build a positive mindset and propel action.

Habits versus rituals

Rituals are different from habits in that you do not think about habits. You brush your teeth every day without having to think about it. By the time you are an adult, the behavior of brushing teeth daily has become automated. The difference with rituals is that they will increase mindfulness.

By definition, rituals are actions whose symbolic meaning goes past their instrumental value. The folding of the American flag is a ritual – it is not about showmanship or easy storage, but the folds have symbolic meaning. A ritual is a celebration that involves your full attention and emotions.

Rituals are specific and detailed. They are easy to repeat and help towards attaining a particular outcome. A ritual helps you prepare for something while a habit is done repeatedly to perform the action in question. You develop a habit without knowing, but you perform rituals deliberately. Rituals require engagement and intent.

Where a habit involves a specific action done repeatedly, a ritual involves many activities and elements – many habits. For example, Mark Twain would enter his study every morning and write until 5 pm. He skipped lunch and did not accept interruptions. After dinner, he would read the work he wrote that day to his family.

Habits are action-oriented – you start them and then keep doing them thoughtlessly. Rituals, on the other hand, are system-oriented. A ritual needs a clear beginning, middle, and end. When rituals become habits, it is because they have a deep meaning for the people involved.

Living within many ritual cycles is vital for your mental health. It helps to deal with feelings of anxiety and destabilization and allows you to create a clear path ahead.

Morning Rituals

Marcus Aurelius is credited with the quote 'When you wake up in the morning, consider the privilege of life – to think, to breathe, to enjoy and to love. '

Generating that positivity in the morning is a sure way to secure any day. In the precious hours of the morning, you set a mindset to carry you throughout the day, so it is vital to treat this period with respect and attention.

Create time to make your morning mindful by creating simple rituals that you can perform in a short time. The idea is to ease into the morning with purpose so that you create an open mind and a clear head to make sure that your day is full of direction, enthusiasm, and positive energy.

Bear in mind that you do not have to adopt all the rituals listed here; you can simply pick a couple that work for you and ensure that you do them consistently enough for them to become a habit.

- Practice gratitude

You can set an attitude of gratitude as you start your day by having a mindset that shows respect and appreciation for what you have and what will happen. Recognizing such emotions will bring more awareness of life. Gratitude is a self-inventory of thankfulness. You can practice it by keeping a gratitude journal. There, note down every morning up to five things that you are grateful for. Once in a while, you can also write gratitude letters to people you care about.

- Meditate

Consistent meditation practices will help you to reduce your stress levels and improve concentration. Meditating in the morning will increase self-awareness and start your day on the right foot. It will increase your happiness, productivity, and performance. If you are just starting, try concentration meditation or mindfulness meditation for five minutes every day. Focus on the thoughts entering your mind and how they influence your emotional state.

- Visualization

Entrepreneurs, top athletes, and highly driven people use visualization. Practicing visualization in the morning will help you to connect your emotions with your long-term and short-term goals. Emotions influence your state of mind and your state of mind will hugely affect the activities you do every day and their outcomes. When visualizing, you want to align the what, how, and why's of your life. It is critical that as you progress towards your goals, you refine and re-evaluate your vision. Feeling good about what you envision is paramount and will help you to keep on track.

- Affirmations

Affirmations are statements that influence your mind to become goal-oriented. It affects your thinking, which in turn affects your behavior, habits, and performance. You can use affirmations to support your visualization activities or use them independently, provided you practice affirmations every morning. It is a plus if the statements align with your vision. Think of the affirmations as the "new codes" that you input into your program. Your subconscious mind takes in the positive statements and gradually uses that to re-condition yourself.

There are different techniques that you can do to increase the effects of your affirmations. First, use the words "I am" or "I choose" at the very start. Don't begin with, "I hope," "I wish," or "I want." These phrases are not as powerful and as confident as "I am" because they entail some levels of uncertainty. Formulate your affirmations with conviction. With that said, create them in such a way that it speaks to the present you. To what you are now. For example, 'I am strong and able to deal with whatever comes at me,' or 'I am beautiful and independent.'

- Exercise

Exercising in the morning can help you to get your day started well. It can set the tone for a healthier day and a happier mindset. When you exercise in the morning, you release cortisol, the hormone that keeps you alert and awake. Typically, the hormone increases in the morning and drops in the evening. Your body is primed to exercise in the morning. Other benefits of exercising in the morning include more overall energy, better mood, and better focus. The cherry on top is that it will support weight loss and appetite control.

- Forgiveness

Every morning, think about the things that you are likely holding on to that other people did that you need to let go of. Forgiveness clears your vision and helps you to face the day without anger and resentment, weighing you down. As you forgive other people, be keen to forgive yourself for the decisions you have made that you no longer feel support your vision.

- Goal setting

You can set aside a few minutes every morning to think about the day and how you want to spend it. Consider everything that needs doing and how the daily activities line up with your overall goal. You want to make sure that as you prepare your to-do list, you are spending time on things that support your vision for your life.

- Listening to or reading uplifting content

Some people listen to inspiring or smart TED talks. Others read motivating articles, quotes, or books to encourage them. You can also choose to listen to a podcast or music that will refocus your mind on what you want to achieve. Pick content that will give you a positive outlook on life. It will open your horizons, which is just what you need as you begin your day.

Before Bed Rituals

After the day, you will need to establish some rituals that will set you up to sleep well and to wake up in the right mood to do it all over again. A positive mindset is something you have to work for, and it may require discipline in the first couple of days, but keep at it. The following are rituals you can set up to do every day before bed:

- Write three things that went well and three that did not

The point here is to audit your day.

Acknowledge everything that went right each day to keep yourself from dwelling on the negative and to monitor the progress that you are making. It is an exercise in gratitude. There is also value in writing what did not go right. It allows you to know the tweaks to make before any problems that might be brewing become disasters. It will enable you to make small improvements daily and to correct your course when there is still time. This exercise should not take more than ten minutes.

- Make a to-do list for the next day

You can make this list as part of your nightly or morning routine. The point is to get a sense of what the next day looks like before you start it. A concise and clear to-do list will give you purpose. If you do it before you go to bed, it will allow your mind to rest – you will not have to worry about the next day. It gives your subconscious mind an opportunity to think about ideas all night. Once you wake up, you will have a clear sense of what the day brings.

- Remove what you need for the next day

Some people cannot go to bed without firmly laying out their clothes for the next day and preparing lunch so that it is ready to grab. The little rituals work like rehearsals for the next day, and they help you to sleep well. Getting the tasks done is also helpful for people whose schedules are so busy that they do not have much time to spare.

The more you can do ahead of schedule, the more prepared you will be to focus on the truly important things of the day. It will allow you to have fewer hitches because you will be prepared before you leave.

- Soak in a bath or take a hot shower

The whole idea of bedtime routines is to allow you to de-stress and relax. There will be days that you will need some more help to calm down and loosen up. A shower or a bath can help with that. Immersion in water is therapeutic and will help you to detach from how hyper-connected technology makes everything feel. Water has a way of relaxing your mind, to make your thoughts fluid and crystallize your ideas.

- Take a walk

Some people cannot go to bed if they did not work out at night. If that is not your kind of thing, consider taking a walk. Walk at a mild pace so that it is relaxing rather than taxing. It will allow your body to unwind and your mind to cool down. It will also give you plenty of space to reflect and provide another perspective that could create new ideas. Allow your thoughts to wander as you stroll.

- Stretch

If you spend most of your days behind a desk, your joints can feel stiff, and your muscles could begin to cramp. You can integrate stretching into your nighttime routine to help you loosen up and get a good night's sleep. Find a quiet space in your home and relegate it to the stretches. Your body will thank you for it.

- Spend time with someone you love

Research shows that the habit of talking over

your day with someone you love can help to de-stress, recharge, swap stories, and reflect. Talking about the things happening in your life helps to develop deep and lasting relationships. You can do this with a family member, friends, or partner. Your brain calms down from the reminder that you are loved.

- Meditate

Meditation will help your mind to be at peace after a chaotic day. It gives you perspective and space to calm down the racing thoughts that rob you of sleep. Note that it will take patience and consistency to master meditation. Your brain is used to distractions and may resist focus. Keep at it, and you will enjoy the rewards.

- Visualization

One of the traits that successful people share is their ability to visualize what success looks like to them. After understanding the place they want to be, they create that image firmly in their mind. When you do this before bed, you solidify your goal in your mind as you sleep. According to Napoleon Hill, this visualization should be your chief aim. It helps to clarify the purpose of your life. It also helps you to affirm the outcome you desire, your biggest dreams, and goals. Doing this before you sleep will activate your subconscious as you sleep. Keep a notepad next to the bed to write down good ideas when you wake up.

- Adequate sleep

Adequate sleep is vital to making sure that you are well equipped to handle the next day. Successful people make sure they rest well.

They know that less than five hours of sleep will leave them exhausted, mentally drained, and grumpy. Sleep deprivation is also connected to stroke, heart disease, and high blood pressure.

The recommended amount of sleep by the National Sleep Foundation is between seven and nine hours every night for adults. Make it a habit to sleep nearly the same time every night so that your body can set up a sleep rhythm and make your sleep invigorating. If you keep to a pattern, your body will be used to it and will give cues when the time is right until you no longer struggle to fall asleep.

- Journaling

Stressing or worrying before bedtime can stop your body from winding down. If it always appears like you get ideas of things to do when you need to be in bed, you may consider journaling to redirect your mind. Journaling will help you capture the thoughts in your mind and to let go of the stress of the day. There is so much information to consume throughout the day, and it is vital to know how to process it. In your journal, write down any thought that comes to mind and any 'great' ideas you might have. Revisit them the next day and see if you think them so great.

In addition, try to answer these questions honestly:

1. What good thing did I do today?
2. What bad thing happened today because of my actions?
3. Can I forgive myself and leave it behind?

You can create other questions for yourself based on the things you value and answer them per day. They will help you to process the day and to see how you interacted with other people all through.

Additional Considerations

Here are a few additional bonus hacks that can add to a good night's sleep.

- Change how you think about sleep

What are the last things you think just before you get into bed? Have you ever thought to yourself that 'I am so exhausted, I will never get enough sleep?' Or perhaps you count the hours you have to sleep and consider them not to be enough. Remember that it is not just your thoughts about life in general that determine your destiny; even what you think about sleep can bring rest or trouble. Reframe your thoughts to positive thoughts and watch that change the way you live.

- Get rid of the blue light

Remove the blue light from the devices in the bedroom. Blue light affects your sleep negatively. Get rid of any alarm clocks or night lights that burn blue and avoid bringing phones and tablets into the bedroom.

- Turn the clock around

When you look at your clock, you start to worry about how little time you have to sleep. It is understandable but avoidable. A simple solution is to have the clock face the other direction.

- Create a different sleeping space for your pet

Animals get restless, and your pet can get in the way of you having proper rest.

<u>Summary</u>

In this chapter, you have learned what makes a ritual and how rituals are different from habits. Rituals are intentional and unite your emotions towards a specific goal. Repeated over time, they could become habits. When trying to develop a positive outlook, rituals will help you to stay focused. They will get rid of inaction and move you toward your goal.

Rituals transform the mundane and allow you to be more mindful. In the morning, start your day on the right foot by:

- Keeping a gratitude journal
- Forgiving yourself and others
- Exercising

- Setting goals
- Visualization
- Meditation and
- Affirming yourself

When the day ends, finish it in style by:

- Meditating
- Journaling
- Taking a walk
- Stretching
- Making a to-do list for the next day
- Planning what you need for the next day and
- Having adequate sleep

Positive Mindset Mastery

Chapter 8: Reaching Your Full Potential

"The only person you are destined to become is the person you decide to be." –Ralph Waldo Emerson

Have you ever felt like you are not living up to your potential? Or perhaps you are unsure whether it is even possible to reach your full potential. If that is you, it means that you are an ambitious person who wants to live their life the best way you know how. That is what it means to reach your potential.

Everyone's time on earth is limited. Some people live longer than others, but it is not about how long you live but what you do with the time you have. It is about living your dreams and aspirations. It is essential to clarify that in the context of this book, reaching your potential is not about living up to the society's or people's expectations of you.

When all is said and done, and you are alone with yourself, are you happy with the choices you have made? When you chase goals and objectives that are not yours (imposed) even if you succeed, your success will be empty. Reaching your potential is about becoming the best version of yourself. That is the goal.

It is a beautiful thing to want to reach your full potential and to strengthen your abilities as much as you can. As a rule of thumb, think through whatever your goal is so that when you know your "why", you will be able to withstand anything that comes your way, including criticism and the judgment of people who do not even know you.

Guard what you believe success to look like from outside influences and from situations where you have to defend it unnecessarily, and remember that Rome was not built in one day. You will need to persist regardless of the unexpected events and setbacks and anything that resists your path. Reaching your potential will require tenacity.

Regardless of the success you have accumulated in life and no matter where you are at, you can always do better. Keep working and keep pushing forward after you hit the goal you are pursuing. With that in mind, the following are seven skills you will need to reach your full potential.

7 Skills to Reach Your Full Potential

1. Self-awareness

Self-awareness is about being comfortable with what you are and where you are in life. It is about giving up any pretenses and impulses to be anyone you are not. When you are self-aware, you do not change yourself simply because other people think you should.

To reach your full potential, you have to know who you are and be proud of it. If you are not aware, you can find out – write, think, talk, and read – they all help you to be mindful of what your thoughts are. When you are self-aware, you will learn more about who you are automatically. Self-knowledge accompanies self-awareness.

2. Leadership

Keep the focus on yourself and work on your problems. You want to become a person who is stable enough to rely on. When you have achieved that, your goal will now be to inspire others to put as much effort into their lives. The best way to do that is to teach people how they can rely on themselves. A leader teaches other people to be independent and sets a good example, and a narcissist wants dependents.

3. Effective communication

Better writing is inevitably connected to better thinking. Better thinking is connected to better communication, which then produces better results in every area of life. If you never thought writing to be important, you can change that now. Start working on improving your writing skills, if you want to express yourself better and begin making connections you never thought possible.

Diction refers to your natural manner of speaking and is a very powerful tool in any society. When interacting with others, it can determine your credibility in their eyes and even whether or not they like you. By working on your diction and speaking ability, you'll be able to speak clearly and with conviction, improve your charisma around others, and emerge as a more self-assured individual.

4. Assertiveness

All of us can think of times when we know we should speak up, but we don't. When we feel like we're being taken advantage of, but we just accept it. Later, we kick ourselves, thinking: "If only I would have said something!"

Being assertive will allow you to stand up for what you believe, ask for what you want and need, and say no to what you don't want in a way that's confident, calm, and respectful.

5. Goal setting

One of the common assumptions people make when they hear about mindfulness is that you will no longer have the drive to pursue goals. The reverse, however, is true. The more present you are, the more you feel compelled to improve your circumstances and to find ways to do that. Just thinking about achieving your goals will not achieve them for you – you have to do the work. You have to set the goals and take action.

Setting goals is about clarifying where you want to be in a specific period. After that, break down what it looks like to be there into activities to do every day. That will help with productivity. You will know what a productive day for you looks like, and the things that deserve your attention.

6. Perseverance

There will be many days that you will want to give up because you will not always see results. What do you do then? You keep working even without the money, recognition, or rewards. You plow ahead and trust the process. In due time, you start to enjoy the results of your hard work. Once this starts to happen, the benefits motivate you further, and you put more effort to reap even more of them in a cycle.

7. Self-development

The importance of self-development often goes unnoticed. We choose to conveniently brush our shortcomings under the carpet. Just as learning should never stop, the same applies to self-improvement. The idea should be to focus on continuous self-development at every stage in our lives and become better versions of ourselves. By choosing to take charge of our development, we are able to reach our full potential and move forward to achieve what we want.

The route to excellence is one of constantly developing oneself. You have to resolve that you will compete against yourself. If you did ten sit-ups in your work out this week, you do 12 the next. The idea is to keep becoming better than you were the previous day. Making that commitment to self-development is the first step on the path to personal fulfillment.

Dream, Believe, and Dare to Do

"In this world, you're either growing or you're dying, so get in motion and grow." –Lou Holtz

Some people believe that you reach your full potential at a specific age. This means that at that age, you are the best you can be, and after that, you are unlikely to get better. Such people could frown at any effort to be better. They might tell you that you are too old to be putting in a certain amount of effort.

Society says that it is only young people who manage to get to their full potential and that the older you get, the fewer the chances you will have. However, this does not have to be true for you – it may be socially accepted, but you do not have to accept it as true.

You can change your life at any age – you do not have to be young to try to get to your goals. It is never too late to unlock your full potential.

There are numerous examples of successful people who only achieved success when they were much older. Age is simply a number that you do not have to allow to hold you back from trying to be better. Think about the following examples:

- Martha Stewart worked in catering for many years before she began hosting her TV show. She started writing her books in her 40s.
- Before Henry Ford was successful, he worked as an engineer, being trained by Thomas Edison. He was 40 years of age

when he founded the Ford Motor company.
- Warren Buffett has made 99.7% of his wealth after the age of 52
- Ray Kroc passed his 50th birthday before he bought the first McDonald's in 1961, which he ultimately expanded into a worldwide conglomerate.
- Sam Walton opened the first Wal-Mart in 1962 when he was 44.

One of the most critical factors to being successful is the belief that you can be successful. If you consistently put yourself down and convince yourself that you cannot reach your potential, the chances are that you will not.

You have to believe in the person that you are and the power you have to get over your limiting beliefs. You are the only thing that is holding you back. Not even the criticism and negative words of other people have that power to get in your way.

Alongside believing that you can reach your full potential, you have to believe also that you deserve the success of doing that. You have to replace any limiting beliefs you have with positive mindsets, so that no matter your age, you are motivated to change your habits and your lifestyle as you watch the negative beliefs fall off.

Dream, believe, and dare to do! You might be positively surprised at what comes out of your efforts.

Summary

Reaching your full potential will require you to put in a little more effort into your life. It will demand that you use skills like:

- Self-awareness
- Leadership
- Goal-setting
- Effective communication
- Mindfulness
- Self-development
- Perseverance

It will demand that you believe in yourself and in your ability to rise above any situation, to dare, to dream, and to do until you have the desires of your heart.

Conclusion

'Optimism does not wait on facts; it deals with prospects.' – Norman Cousins

Like optimism, a positive mindset is not a slave to the circumstances.

It could be the difference between success and failure, progress and stagnation in any area of your life. It can help you to avoid stress and to even out any devastating and challenging situation coming your way by allowing you to see the silver lining.

Every challenge becomes an opportunity for you to learn and to grow. You can accept reality and try to make the best of it. A positive mindset can help you to avoid mental and physical diseases. When you no longer give weight to the negative thoughts, your body does not experience the discomfort of worry, stress, frustration, and anxiety. According to research, there are undeniable connections between a stress-free life and a stronger immune system.

Most of the battles that you face in life can be won if you are confident in your abilities. When you have a positive mindset, confidence simply oozes out of you. You reconfigure your personality and perform at your best, which boosts your self-esteem and the knowledge that you can make the proper decisions at the appropriate time, confidently.

As demonstrated in this book, a positive mindset will benefit every area of your life and not just your career. Positivity is rooted in gratitude for the things you have, and it will always add happiness to those around you. By expressing appreciation and gratitude, you strengthen bonds and allow yourself to enjoy a satisfying life.

A positive attitude in life is an investment that continually pays off. You start by confronting things that get in the way of the mindset, leaning on techniques to do better, and developing daily rituals to cement it. Soon, a new attitude takes over, and you no longer have to think about it; it happens subconsciously.

It should be clear that achieving that positive attitude is not an impulse. There is no elixir, magic pill, or short cut towards changing your outlook. This is what makes the journey inherently rewarding. The icing on the cake is that a positively changed life is rooted in unlimited gratitude that you can practice for the rest of your life and whose benefits you will continue to reap.

It says a lot about how far you are in the process that you have chosen to read this book. You are well on your way to becoming a better you.

All the best in your efforts!

REFERENCES

1. *The Power of Positive Thinking*. (1956).
2. Gillespie, M.P. (1995). *The picture of Dorian gray: "what the world thinks me"*. Macmillan Reference USA.
3. Emerson, R. W., & Tilton, E. M. (1939). *The letters of Ralph Waldo Emerson*. Columbia University Press.
4. Kolbert, E. (2014). *The sixth extinction: An unnatural history*. A&C Black.
5. Johnson, D.M (2011). Socrates and Athens. Cambridge University Press.
6. *12 ways to raise a competent, confident child with grit*. (2015, 5). Psychology Today. https://www.psychologytoday.com/us/blog/peaceful-parents-happy-kids/201506/12-ways-raise-competent-confident-child-grit
7. *Optimism may reduce risk of dying prematurely among women*. (2020, March 28). News. https://www.hsph.harvard.edu/news/press-releases/optimism-premature-death-women/
8. Santos-Longhurst, A. (n.d.). *How to think positive and have an optimistic outlook: 8 tips*. Healthline. https://www.healthline.come/health/how-to-think-positive
9. *What is positive mindset: 89 ways to achieve a positive mental attitude*. (2019, December 20). PositivePsychology.com.

https://positivepsychology.com/positive-mindest/
10. 6. *Goal setting theory – PSYCH 484: Work attitudes and job motivation – Confluence. (n.d.). WikiSpaces* – Confluence. Retrieved July 12, 2020, from https://WikiSpaces.psu.edu/display/PSYCH484/6.+Goal+Setting+Theory
11. *Daily rituals: Create a positive mindset for a happier life. (n.d.).* Liora. https://liorabels.com/daily-rituals-create-a-positive-mindset-for-a-happier-life/
12. *What mindset rituals do you do daily to improve the quality of your life? (*2018, January 19). Viral Solutions – Your Personal Chief Marketing Officer. https://viralsolutions.net/what-mindset-rituals-do-you-do-daily-to-improve-the-quality-of-your-life/#.XxUyG8gzbIV
13. *The power of rituals: How to build meaningful habits – Gustavo Razzetti.* (2020, February 25). Liberationist – Change Leadership. https://liberationist.org/the-power-of-rituals-how-to-build-meaningful-habits/
14. LeMind, A., & B.A. (2013, August 8). *8 simple techniques to persuade and influence people.* Learning Mind. https://www.learning-mind.com/8-simple-techniques-to-persuade-and-influence-people/
15. Lee, B. (1998). *The power principle: Influence with honor. Simon &Schuster.*
16. *8 tips for developing positive relationships.* (2013, March 21). Training Magazine/

professionals. https://trainingmag.com/content/8-tips-developing-positive-relationships/
17. Anthony, K. (n.d.). *EFT tapping*. Healthline. https://www.healthline.com/health/eft-tapping
18. *7 essential beliefs for leadership success*. (2016, July 4). Leadership Freak. https://leadershipfreak.blog/2016/07/03/7-essential-beliefs-for-leadership-success/
19. Cre8veonline.com. (n.d.). *Anchoring – NLP technique: : NLP-secrets.com*. Upgrade Your Mind with Neuro-Linguistic Programing (NLP), Body Language and Hypnosis. https://www.nlp-secrets.com/nlp-technique-anchoring.php
20. Gill, B. (2017, June 22). *New to visualization? Here are 5 step to get you started*. Forbes. https://www.forbes.com/sites/bhaligill/2017/06/22/new-to-visualization-here-are-5-steps-to-get-you-started/#5c8c80ef6e3f
21. Laozi, Wieger, L., Liezi, Zhuangzi, & Bryce, D. (1984). *Wisdom of the Daoist masters: The works of Lao Zi (Lao tzu), lie Zi (Lieh tzu), Zhung Zi (Chuang tzu)*.
22. Gold, L. H., & Simon, R. I. (2015). *Gun violence and mental illness*. American Psychiatric Pub.
23. Johnson, R. A. (2009). *Inner work: Using dreams and active imagination for personal growth*. HarperCollins.
24. Hockenbury, D., & Hockenbury, S.E. (2012). *Discovering psychology*. Worth Publishers.

25. Darwin, C. (2013). *The expression of the emotions in man and animals*. Courier Corporation.

HOW TO STOP BEING NEGATIVE, ANGRY, AND MEAN

Master Your Mind and Take Control of Your Life

Richard Banks

Positive Mindset Mastery

INTRODUCTION

"Once you replace negative thoughts with positive ones, you'll start having positive results." – Willie Nelson

All you have to do is look around the world and see that there is no shortage of negativity. This can make it extremely hard for a person who strives to be positive to make a positive impact on themselves and others. The truth of the matter is, we are all going to encounter negative circumstances and people throughout our lives. Unless we can learn how to manage these things effectively, we will forever remain prisoners in our lives instead of taking control of our own destiny. That's what this book is here to do.

Let me ask you something, how often over the last two weeks have you felt angry, out of control, or down? Hopefully, you haven't felt these things that often, but there is probably a good chance you have. If you hadn't, then you probably wouldn't be here right now. Just know, if these feelings are ever-present in your life, or at least feel as if they are, you are not alone. The good news is, those feelings can be transformed.

Everybody gets angry now and then, but some seem to stay angry, or at least get mad more often than others and lose control. This book will help you to get rid of that rage that often comes with anger. Additionally, this book will help people who are looking to have more control over their anger and emotions in general. These proven techniques can change your life forever. Just imagine not allowing your anger to take control of your life. When you use these techniques within the book, you will learn how to stop your anger in its tracks, and you will soon find that you are a much happier and positive person. You will know how to deal with your anger, instead of falling prey to it. You can use that energy to fulfill something in your life in a constructive way.

As an advocate for mental health, mindfulness, and positivity, I have scoured many studies and techniques and applied them to my own life, to figure out what helps and what doesn't. This, along with the years of experience, I truly understand the importance of mindset and psychology, and the role they play in achieving a person's goals and how they cope with disappointment, change, and stress.

This book is for people who have tried many other techniques and methods to control the anger and negative thinking but failed. This book will teach you how to set yourself free. You will discover the reasons for your anger. Then you will find that those negative feelings lose the grip they have over you.

After reading through this book, you will find that you are more aware of the power you have always had. You will have steps that you can take to improve yourself, and skills to use to rewire your brain to reach a healthier mind. You will no longer be caught off-guard by the negative sides of life. Ultimately, What you THINK leads to how you FEEL, and What you

FEEL leads to how you BEHAVE.

With my help and expertise, you will have the knowledge and skills you need to change your mindset and grow as a person. Now, I'm not telling you that the information I will provide you in this book is a magical cure-all pill for happiness, but it will help you to grow. This book is focused on helping you start your mental health journey.

The great thing is, is the brain is malleable and can be changed. It also doesn't take a lot of tools to change the brain. All you need to do is be more aware of your internal dialogue and change it to something more positive and healthier. Why wait any longer? Let's get started and learn precisely how to be a more positive and happier person.

Positive Mindset Mastery

Chapter 1: Thoughts Vs. Core Beliefs

If you were to Google "thought," you are going to get a bunch of circular, uninformative information and definitions like "an idea or opinion produced by thinking or occurring suddenly in the mind." Merriam-Webster defines the word "think" as "to form or have in the mind." Neither of those definitions really tells us what a thought is.

When you have a thought, it represents something you have experienced. That representation is a likeness of the original experience. The representation that you have created in your mind has similar characteristics of the original experience. For example, a mold, imprint, image, or picture of an object is a representation of the original item.

Thoughts

Thoughts are fundamentally just "maps" that correspond to a person's external environment.

Some scientists suggest that all thoughts are built upon analogy –making. The brain can detect similarities between new information and previous information, which enables the use of previously learned information to something new (Lewis, 2019).

People have automatic thoughts throughout the day as they make sense of what is going on.

In a therapy setting, clients can get help to identify these automatic thoughts by asking things like:

- What do others say about this?
- What does this mean for you?
- What was going through your mind at that moment?

Some automatic thoughts have greater importance than others to understand what is going on in a person's mind. Recording these thoughts can give a person a better understanding of when automatic thoughts happen.

Core Beliefs

A core belief is a central belief that a person holds about their self, the world, and others. Core beliefs tend to be formed early on in life and can refer to a cognitive construct like "I am unlovable" or "people can't be trusted." When a person feels anxious, it is common for the core belief "I am weak" to be activated. If they were in less threatening situations, the core belief "I am strong" could be activated. When they are activated, the person experiences the beliefs as absolute truths.

There are times when people with depression or anxiety will develop strong core beliefs that aren't balanced through other core beliefs. In a therapy setting, one way to detect core beliefs is to notice thoughts that come along with a strong emotion that doesn't shift in the face of contrasting evidence (Lewis, 2019).

Let's look at an example:

Two students just took a test, and they both fail the test.

Person A's core belief is "I am a failure." Their reaction to this failed test would start with the thought, "Of course I failed... why bother?" This makes them feel depressed, and they don't do anything to change.

Person B's core belief is, "I am perfectly capable when I give my best effort." Their reaction to this failed test would start with the thought, "I did poorly because I didn't prepare." They would feel disappointed, and they would plan on studying harder before the next test.

One of the main challenges of changing your thought processes is being able to let them go. A possible explanation for this is that there could be a strong core belief at the root of that unhelpful thought. Core beliefs tend to be inflexible, rigid, and strongly-held beliefs that are maintained through the tendency to focus on the information that reinforced the belief and ignoring anything that contradicts it.

Not all core beliefs are inherently bad, but there is a good chance that you have some harmful core beliefs. These are those beliefs that are hidden beneath the surface-level. For example, a core belief of "nobody likes me" could lie under the belief, "my friends only spend time with me out of pity."

Some other harmful core beliefs include:

- Helpless beliefs: "I am weak," "I'm a loser," "I am trapped."
- Unlovable beliefs: "I am unlovable," "I will end up alone," "No one likes me."
- Worthless beliefs: "I am bad," "I don't deserve to live," "I am worthless."

- External danger beliefs: "The world is dangerous," "People can't be trusted," "Nothing ever goes right."

These types of core beliefs have consequences. Mentally, they could cause low self-esteem, difficulty handling stress, substance abuse, anxiety, and depression. It can also affect your relationships, such as:

- Placing the needs of others before your own.
- Being overly aggressive or confrontational.
- Being overly jealous.
- Feeling inadequate in relationships.
- Difficulty trusting other people.

Since these core beliefs are learned, they can also be unlearned. Also, if the core belief is negative, there is a good chance that it is wrong, even if it feels right.

Perception

"A map is not the territory it represents, but, if correct, it has a similar structure to the territory, which accounts for its usefulness." — Alfred Korzybski,

In the world of semantics, as stated by Alfred Korzybski, we have a world outside, and then we have five senses that we use to perceive the world. We use our five senses to create a representation of the world, and that's how we see things. It is our internal representation of the world, which is different from everybody else's. This is what is called the map. The map is not the territory, just like your perception of the world is not the world (Marta, 2014).

If you are in a very emotional situation between you and somebody else, you have a perception of what's going on within you. You know who started it, who's to blame, but it may not be the same perception as the other person's. There could be a lot of drama, and your perception of it is not the actual situation. It's subjective.

The problem is, we often act as if the map is the territory. This is why we should have just enough self-doubt so that no matter what your reaction is, you realize it's still subjective. You understand that you could learn a little more about the situation. You may recognize that the other person's point of view could be helpful. Maybe in the heat of the moment, when you are sure, you could stop and look at yourself and think about what is going on because your programming is involved.

We all want to make any relationship we have work, whether personal or professional, but the inferences that we make in certain situations tend to be inaccurate. Due to these inaccuracies, they cause us to act in ways that could be damaging to the relationship. It's important to keep the understanding that no matter what you think about a situation, it could be wrong.

Let's look at an example. If you saw a spider crawling up the wall right next to you, would you react? Most of you would say yes. This is what is known as the fight-or-flight reaction. Some people would run out of the room, and maybe some would try to fight the spider, but there is going to be some kind of reaction to it.

In this situation, the spider is the stressor, and you are the stressee. But, this is where perception comes into play. You realize that you didn't have your glasses on, and you take a second look and realize it was just a leaf. It only looked like a spider, but it wasn't one. In that sense, did the leaf cause you stress? Was the leaf the stressor? It was your perception that it was a spider that caused you to react.

Here's another example. People can get easily stressed out over time. They perceive their situation as if they don't have enough time to get everything done. They let the worry about time stress them out until they are frazzled, angry, anxious, or a whole host of other negative emotions. But you must learn to look at these things in a different light. Sure, some stress can help motivate you to get things done, but too much stress will hold you back. When simple pressure that you have to get something done by its deadline turns into feelings of being overwhelmed, then it defeats its purpose as a motivator.

In this process of perception, there are three main parts. The first is the external event. This is the thing you are perceiving. It could be a person, a place, an object, or whatever else you experience. The second is the neural associations. When something on the outside happens to you, your brain makes neural associations with it. This is where you can say this happens, and then I react like this. You will start to notice reactive patterns. That's the third thing, your reactive frame. The reactive frame is how you frame the situation or how you experience it. These things happen automatically (Marta, 2014).

For example, if a person yells at you, your reaction to it could be to become indignant and upset with the person. But, if you take a step and reframe the situation, you could say, "They are having a bad day, so it could be why they talked to me like that." You can also start thinking about what you can do to let them know you would rather them not talk to you in that tone of voice. If you are able to look at that person differently, you won't experience that physical reaction.

Cognitive Distortions

"I just failed my math test. I'm not good at school. I might as well just drop out."

"I have the worst luck in the world."

"How do we know it would even work?"

"I'm not a creative person."

All of these are great examples of cognitive distortions. They are thought patterns that cause a person to view reality in an inaccurate way, which is usually negative. They are habitual errors in thinking. When you have cognitive distortion, the way you interpret something is usually negatively biased.

We all experience cognitive distortions at times. But when we end up reinforcing them regularly, they can increase anxiety, cause problems in relationships, deepen depression, and lead to many other issues.

Research has found that people develop these distortions as a way to cope with adverse life events. The more severe and prolonged those events are, the greater the odds are that one or more of these distortions are going to form. One of the earliest theories suggests that humans may have developed these distortions as an evolutionary survival method.

Stress can make a person adapt their thinking in

ways that are helpful to their immediate survival. But most of these thoughts aren't healthy or rational long-term.

Researchers have found that there are at least ten common cognitive distortions.

1. Polarized Thinking

This is often referred to as black and white thinking. This distortion happens typically when a person habitually thinks in extremes. When you think that you are either going to succeed or doomed to fail, that people are either good or bad, you engage in this type of thinking.

2. Overgeneralization

When a person overgeneralizes, they conclude a single event, and then they incorrectly apply their conclusion towards everything. For example, they can make a bad grade on a test and conclude that they just suck in that class. They have a terrible experience in a relationship and assume all relationships are going to be like that.

3. Catastrophizing

This type of thinking causes a person to dread or assume the worst when they are facing something unknown. This causes ordinary worries to escalate quickly. For example, you don't get a check that you were expecting, and you catastrophize that you will never get it and that you won't be able to pay any of your bills, and your family will be evicted.

It's easy to dismiss this as an overreaction, but those who have developed this cognitive distortion might have experienced repeated adverse problems so often that they always fear the worst.

4. Personalization

This is the most common error in thinking, and that is taking things personally when they aren't even connected to you at all. This distortion can come up when you blame yourself for a situation that isn't your fault or was out of your control. Another example was when you incorrectly assume that you were intentionally targeted or excluded. It is often connected to depression or anxiety.

5. Mind Reading

This is when people assume that they know what others are thinking. This can be hard to distinguish from empathy, which is the ability to understand and perceive what others feel. To spot the difference, it would be helpful to look at the evidence, and not just what confirms your beliefs.

6. Mental Filtering

This is the tendency to ignore the positive and focus only on the negatives. When you interpret a circumstance with a negative filter, it is inaccurate and worsens depression and anxiety.

7. Discounting Positives

Much like mental filters, this involved a negative bias in thinking. Instead of ignoring the positives, they explain them away as a fluke or luck. They don't acknowledge the good outcome as skill, determination, or a smart choice. They simply assume that it had to have been an accident or anomaly.

8. Self-serving bias

This is the tendency to blame external forces when bad things happen and give yourself credit when good things happen. For example, when you win a poker hand, it is due to your skill at reading the other players and knowing the odds, while when you lose, it is due to getting dealt a poor hand.

9. Confirmation bias

This is favoring information that conforms to your existing beliefs and discounting evidence that does not conform.

10. Labeling

This is a distortion where people reduce themselves or others to a single, negative descriptor, such as a failure or a drunk. Labeling can make a person berate. This misperception can cause some major problems between people.

The good news is that all of this can be fixed, and cognitive distortions can be eradicated.

Recap

Remember that your thoughts are created through the mix of stimuli and your core beliefs. While controlling your thoughts may difficult, it is not impossible. Your thoughts can change your life, so you must learn how to change your thought processes.

Chapter 2: Emotions

Emotions and thoughts are related, and we can experience them at the same time, but they are very different. Let's look a bit closer to see exactly what they are.

Emotions

It might help you if you think of emotions as an experience and flow of feelings like fear, anger, sadness, or joy. Emotions have an innate ability to be triggered by external or internal stimuli. External stimuli might be from watching a sad movie or seeing a friend suffer from a disease like cancer. Internal stimuli might happen when you remember something sad.

Even though emotions are universal, everyone is going to experience and respond to them differently. Some might struggle with figuring out which emotion they are experiencing.

Emotions are there to help us connect with others and to help create strong bonds socially. People who can build strong emotional ties and bonds become part of a community and are more likely to find protection and support that is needed to survive.

People all over the world will have different thoughts, opinions, beliefs, and ideas, but most people will have the same feelings.

What Can Influence Our Emotions?

Research has shown that emotions can be contagious. Humans have a tendency to mimic another person's outward state like when you pass someone in the grocery store, and they smile, you automatically smile back at them no matter what you might be feeling inward. Our outward state can affect our internal states, too, such as smiling could really make you feel happier.

Other factors that can influence emotions:

- Physical Conditions

Thyroid disorders, Alzheimer's, Multiple Sclerosis, Parkinson's Disease, strokes, brain tumors, and metabolic diseases like diabetes can cause someone's emotional responses to change drastically.

- Genetics

To get a bit more specific here, personality and brain structure, including one's self-control, can affect their emotional expression. Even though a person's genetics can't be changed, the brain is a completely different story. There are six definite "emotional styles" that get based on the structure of the brain, but we can reshape them with some practice.

- Cultural Beliefs and Traditions

These can affect how a person or group of people express their emotions. Some cultures deem it as "bad manners" if you express your emotions in ways that might not be considered appropriate and healthy in another culture.

The Things We Think Can Impact the Things We Feel

Emotions and thoughts have a huge effect on each other. Our thoughts can trigger an emotion. It can also help you look at the emotion. Let's say you have a job interview in a couple of days, and you might begin feeling a bit scared. You can tell yourself that what you are feeling isn't a realistic fear.

Additionally, the way we appraise and attend to our lives can have an impact on the way we feel. If you have a fear of dogs, you will probably be a bit more attentive to the dog who lives across the street from you. You watch them very closely when they begin approaching you. You automatically start feeling threatened, and this can lead to some emotional distress. Someone else sees the dog coming, and the view them as being friendly, and they have an entirely different emotional response about the same situation.

Can Emotions and Thoughts Be Changed?

We like believing that our emotions are just one more part of who we are, and they can't be changed. Research has shown that emotions are pliable. This means that they can be changed. Here are a few ways you can change them:

- By changing an external situation. For example, leaving an abusive partner.
- By changing your attention. For example, deciding to focus on a positive aspect of any given situation.
- By reframing the situation. For example, an upcoming test is an opportunity for you to learn and not an assessment of your worth.

The way you choose to live your life has massive power over how you feel each day. Specific kinds of mental training like positive thinking or mindfulness could affect how we look at the world and can help us feel happier, more resilient, and calmer. Other studies have found several other attitudes like kindness, gratitude, and forgiveness that can be practiced and cultivated (Lawson, n.d.).

Defense Mechanisms

Defense mechanisms are behaviors that people use to remove themselves from unpleasant thoughts, actions, or events. These are psychological strategies that might help you put distance between yourself and the unwanted feelings or threats like shame or guilt.

Sigmund Freud first proposed the psychoanalytic theory, and it has evolved with time and says behaviors like defense mechanisms aren't under our control. Most people will do them without even realizing they are using them.

Defense mechanisms are a natural, normal part of psychological development. Being able to identify the different types of defense mechanisms could help you with your future encounters and conversations.

There are several common defense mechanisms. Dozens have been found, but some get used a lot more than others. In many cases, these responses aren't under a person's control. This means you can't control "what you do when you do it." Here are the most common defense mechanisms:

- Denial

This is the most common defense mechanism. It happens when you won't accept facts or reality. You will block external circumstances or events from your mind so you won't have to deal with an emotional impact. You stay away from painful events or feelings.

This defense mechanism is the most widely one that is known, too. You will often hear the phrase: "They are in denial." This is understood to mean that a person is avoiding their reality despite what might be blatantly obvious to everyone else around them.

- Intellectualization

Any time you have been hit with a situation that is trying, you might decide to get rid of all the emotions from your responses and try to focus on just the facts. You might see someone use this strategy when someone loses a job, and they decide to spend their days making spreadsheets about leads and job opportunities.

- Compartmentalization

This happens when you separate your life into separate sectors. This might feel like you are protecting several elements about it.

Let's say you decided not to discuss your personal life at work, so you block off (compartmentalize) that part of your life. This lets you live your life without having to face the challenges or anxieties when you are in a specific mindset or setting.

- Reaction Formation

Anyone who uses this defense mechanism might see how they feel, but they decide to behave oppositely.

Anyone who reacts like this might feel they shouldn't ever express negative emotions like frustration or anger. Instead, they decide to respond in an extremely positive way.

- Sublimation or Redirection

This defense mechanism is thought of as a positive strategy. This is because the people who rely on it have decided to redirect their strong feelings or emotions into an activity or object that is safe and appropriate.

Rather than lashing out at an employee, you decide to funnel your frustration into exercise or kickboxing. You could also redirect or channel your feelings into sports, art, or music.

- Rationalization

Some people might try to explain their undesirable behaviors with a set of "facts." This lets them feel comfortable with the choice that they made, even if they know that it isn't right.

Let's say that a person gets turned down for a date. They may rationalize the situation by saying that they weren't attracted to the person anyway.

- Regression

If a person feels anxious or threatened, they might unconsciously "escape" into an earlier time in their life.

This kind of defense mechanism might be seen more in younger children. If they experience loss or trauma, they might act like they are young again. They might even start sucking their thumb or wetting the bed.

It can happen with Adults also. Adults who have a hard time coping with behaviors or events might start sleeping with a favorite stuffed animal, chewing on pens or pencils, chain-smoking, overeating comfort foods. They might stop doing their daily activities because they feel too overwhelming.

- Displacement

This is when you direct strong frustrations and emotions toward an object or person that isn't threatening to you. This lets you satisfy your impulses to react, but you don't want to risk the consequences.

One good example is getting angry at your partner or child just because you had a rough day at work. Neither one is the cause of your strong emotions, but reacting to them won't bring as many repercussions as blowing up at your boss would.

- Projection

Some feelings or thoughts that you have about someone else might make you feel uncomfortable. If you project these feelings, you are misdirecting them to someone else.

For example, a bully may project their own feelings of vulnerability onto a smaller, weaker target.

- Repression

Irrational beliefs, painful memories, or unsavory thoughts might upset you. Rather than facing them, you might unconsciously decide to hide them, hoping you forget about them altogether.

This isn't saying that your memories are going to disappear. They might influence your behaviors, and they might impact your relationships in the future. You need to realize the impact that this defense mechanism is having on you.

How to Be the Boss of Your Emotions

Being able to express and experience emotions is very important. As a response that is felt in any given situation, emotions can play a huge part in how you react. If you are in tune with them, you will have access to some critical knowledge that can help with:

- Self-care
- Daily interactions
- Successful relationships

- Making decisions

Even though emotions can help you with your life each day, they could hurt your interpersonal relationships and emotional health when they begin feeling out of control.

Any emotion, including positive ones, can be intensified until it becomes hard to control. With some practice, you can rein them in. Research has suggested that having the skills to regulate your emotions has been linked to our well being. They also found a possible link between financial success and these skills; working on that part might pay off literally.

Here are some suggestions to help you get started:

- Know When to Show Emotions

There is a time and place for everything, and this includes intense emotions. Uncontrollably sobbing is a normal response to losing someone you love. Punching and screaming into your pillow may help relieve some of your tension and anger when you get dumped.

Other situations need some restraint. It doesn't matter how frustrated you may be, screaming at your boss over cutting your hours isn't going to help.

You need to be mindful of where you are and the situation. This can help you know when it is fine to express your feelings or if you need to sit still and think about your feelings for some time.

- Breathe Deeply

There is a lot to be said for how powerful breath can be, whether you are so upset that you can't speak or if you are ridiculously happy. Slow down and pay attention to your breathing. Some deep breathing exercises could help you take a step back from the intense emotions and allow you to get grounded so you can avoid any extreme reactions.

The next time your emotions begin taking control:

- Inhale slowly; deep breaths will come from your diaphragm and not the chest. It might help you to imagine your breath coming up from deep inside your belly.
- Hold the breath for a three count and then exhale slowly.

- o Think about a mantra. Some find that repeating a mantra can be helpful, something simple like: "I am relaxed." "I am calm."

- Get Some Space

Putting some distance between you and your feelings could help you react to them reasonably. This distance could be physical, like walking away from a situation that upset you. You could distract yourself by creating some mental distance.

You don't ever want to avoid or block your feelings completely, but it won't hurt you to distract yourself until you are in a place where you can deal with them better. Just be sure you come back to them. Any healthy distraction will just be temporary. You can try:

1. Spend time with your pet
2. Talk to someone you trust
3. Watch a funny video
4. Take a walk

- Get Control of Your Stress

If you are under a lot of stress, handling your emotions might be harder. People who are usually in control of their emotions might find it harder to handle them when they are under stress or a lot of tension.

Finding ways to manage your stress or reducing your stress might help you manage your emotions. Mindfulness practices such as meditation could help relieve stress, too. It isn't going to get rid of it entirely, but it could make it easier to deal with.

Here are some other ways to help you cope with stress:

1. Take time to do your hobbies
2. Take time to relax
3. Spend time in nature
4. Exercise
5. Make time to laugh and talk with close friends
6. Get an adequate amount of sleep

- Meditate

If you already practice meditation, this might be your best method for handling your extreme feelings. Meditation helps you increase your awareness of all your experiences and emotions. While meditating, you will be teaching yourself how to sit still with those feelings. You will be able to see them without making them go away, trying to change them, or judging yourself.

Learning to accept your emotions can make regulating them easier. Meditation can help increase these acceptance skills. It offers you other benefits, too, such as helping you sleep better and relaxing you.

- Keep a Journal

Writing about your feelings and the responses that they trigger could help you to identify patterns. There are times when it might be enough to trace those emotions back through those thoughts. Putting your feelings onto paper can let you reflect on them on a deeper level.

It can help you see when certain circumstances

contribute to emotions that are harder to control. Finding those triggers can make it possible to find ways to manage them better.

Journaling can give you the best benefits when you do it each day. Keep it with you and write down any intense feelings or emotions when they happen. Make sure you write down the triggers and then how you reacted to it. If the reaction didn't help, write in your journal to find things that will be more helpful for your future.

- Accept All of Your Emotions

If you want to manage your emotions better, you could try downplaying your feelings. If you tend to collapse to the floor sobbing and to scream when you can't find your keys, or you hyperventilate when you get good news, it might help you to tell yourself: "It isn't a big deal, so stop freaking out." or "Just calm down."

This won't work. It is invalidating your experience because, to you, it is a huge deal. Accepting your emotions as they come up helps you become comfortable with them. When you can increase your comfort level around these intense emotions, it will let you feel them entirely without reacting in unhelpful or extreme ways.

To practice accepting your emotions, you can try thinking about them as messengers. They aren't bad or good. They are only neutral. They might bring up some unpleasant feelings every now and then, but they are still giving you information that you can use.

You could try something like:

"I am upset because I keep losing my keys, and this makes me late. I should put a dish on the shelf by the door, so I remember to leave them in the same place."

When you accept your emotions, you will be able to find more positivity and fewer mental health problems. This can lead to more happiness over all.

- Identify Your Feelings

Take a few minutes to check in about your mood. This can help you gain control. Let's say you have been dating for a few months. You tried to plan a date last week, but they told you they didn't have the time. You texted them yesterday: "I'd like to see you soon. Can you meet this week?"

They respond 24 hours later: "Busy. Can't."

You get upset suddenly. Without thinking about what you are doing, you hurl your phone into the wall, knock over your trash can, and kick your chair, breaking your toe.

You can interrupt yourself by asking yourself these questions:

1. "What am I feeling right now?" furious, confused, or disappointed
2. "What happened to cause these feelings?" They ignored me without explaining why.
3. "Does this situation have a different explanation that makes sense?" They might have been stressed, sick, dealing

with something that they don't want to explain to you. They may be planning on telling you more later.

4. "What do I want to do about these feelings?" throw things, scream, text them back something rude.
5. "Is there a better way to cope with them?" Ask them if everything is fine. Ask them the next time they will be free. Get some exercise.

When you think about all the possible alternatives, you will be reframing your thoughts. This can help you change your extreme reactions.

It might take some time before you can turn it into a habit. With some practice, doing these steps in your head will get easier.

- **Stop Repressing Try to Regulate**

Your emotions don't have a dial. But just imagine that you were able to manage your emotions by turning a dial. You wouldn't put them on maximum all day long. You wouldn't turn them completely off either.

Any time you repress or suppress your emotions, you are keeping yourself from expressing and experiencing these feelings. This might happen consciously or unconsciously. Consciously would be a suppressed emotion; unconsciously would be a repressed emotion.

Either one of these can lead to physical or mental health problems like:

- Substance abuse

- Difficulty managing stress
- Pain and muscle tension
- Sleep problems
- Depression
- Anxiety

When you are learning to gain control over your emotions, be sure you aren't trying to sweep them under the rug. Healthily expressing your emotions involves finding a balance between no emotions and overwhelming emotions.

- **Look at Your Emotional Impact**

Having intense emotions isn't bad. Emotions can make your lives vibrant, unique, and exciting. Having strong feelings can show that we are embracing life fully, and we aren't suppressing normal reactions.

It is normal to experience some overwhelming feeling occasionally. If something great happens, if something terrible happens, if you feel like you have been missing out.

How will you know if there is a problem?

Any emotion that constantly gets out of hand could lead to:

- Emotional or physical outbursts
- Using illegal substances to manage emotions
- Problems at school or work
- Hard time relating to other people
- Friendship or relationship conflicts

Take the time to figure out how your emotions are affecting your daily life. This makes it easier to find your problem areas.

- Find a Therapist

If you have tried all the above tips and your emotions are still overwhelming you, it might be time to find professional support. Persistent or long-term mood swings and not being able to regulate your emotions have been linked to specific mental health problems, including bipolar disorder and borderline personality disorder. Problems controlling your emotions could relate to family problems, trauma, or other problems.

A therapist can offer judgment-free and compassionate support while you:

    o Practice reframing and challenging the feelings that cause you distress.

- Learn how to play limited emotional expressions up or downplay intense feelings.
- Address any severe mood swings
- Look at all the factors that contribute to your inability to regulate your emotions

Intense emotions and mood swings could provoke unwanted or negative thoughts that could eventually trigger feelings of despair or hopelessness.

This cycle might lead to unhelpful methods of coping, such as self-harm or suicidal thoughts. If you start thinking about committing suicide, or have the urge to harm yourself, talk to someone you trust who could help you find some support immediately.

Recap

You can't continue letting your emotions rule you. When you do, your emotions will dictate the things that you do, and that's going to end up causing you to miss out on things you want to do. Start identifying what you feel so that you can better understand your emotions. From there, try journaling or any of the other activities we have discussed. If you find that you can't get a grasp on your emotions on your own, get in touch with a therapist so that you can get the help that you need.

Emotions are not easy to control, but always remember that you are not your emotions. You always have a choice.

Positive Mindset Mastery

Chapter 3: Shifting Your Mindset

Why do some people shine in any circumstances that they decide to exert themselves, but other people can't manage a glimmer despite obvious talents? Research has shown that it is how they think about their abilities that count the most.

Most people who have reached greatness have worked very hard to get where they are. Most were told that wouldn't ever amount to anything, but they still believed in themselves and worked hard to accomplish it.

Growth vs. Fixed Mindset

There are two different ways to look at ability or intelligence:

- Fixed Mindset: A person's ability and skills are ingrained or fixed. This means that we have been born with a specific ability level, and we won't ever be able to change it.

- Growth Mindset: We can develop our abilities through a lot of effort, hard work, and persistence. Persons with a Growth Mindset believe everyone can get better if they work at it.

The benefits of a growth mindset might seem obvious, but most of us are guilty of having a fixed mindset in certain situations. That can be dangerous because a fixed mindset can often prevent skill development and growth, which could sabotage your health and happiness down the line.

The varying beliefs can result in different behaviors, and ultimately different outcomes. Studies show that students who have a growth mindset can increase their grades with time; however, the ones who believed their intelligence was innate couldn't. Their grades actually got worse over time.

Believing that you are in complete control over your abilities can help you improve and learn. This is the true key to success.

Persistence, effort, and hard work are critical, but they aren't as important as believing that you are in complete control over your destiny.

People who have these mindsets will think differently and react differently to information. They will respond to information about their performance differently.

- People who have a fixed mindset, their brain will be the most active when they get information about how they performed, like on a test or their grades.

- People who have a growth mindset, their brain will be the most active while they are being told the things they can do to do better.

It is an extremely different approach from thinking, "How did I do?" to "What can I do better next time?"

The fixed mindset is more concerned about the

results and the way they are looked at, and the growth mindset is more concerned about development and the ways they can improve. It should be obvious which one will lead to them having a better future.

Handling Setbacks

Mindsets can cause people to handle their setbacks differently.

- People who have a growth mindset look at setbacks as a way to learn. They will generally try harder to overcome their problems.

- People who have a fixed mindset get discouraged by their setbacks since any setback will deplete how they view their abilities. They usually become disinterested and give up.

Brain Plasticity

Do you realize that your brain can change? The old saying that "old dogs can't learn new tricks" isn't true.

The brain is very plastic. It can be molded and reshaped with time to form new pathways. This is why neuroscientists call this neuroplasticity. Neuroplasticity was once thought to occur only during childhood, but research in the latter half of the 20th century showed that many aspects of the brain can be altered even through adulthood.

These pathways get created by thinking or doing certain things. What we say or do can become hard-wired into our brains and turn into habits. These create routes that are very defined in our brains, and they become a part of our internal program. Neural plasticity is the ability of these pathways in the brain to change through growth and reorganization.

This is good news because now you know that you can change your mindset and your internal programming. The first step would be to realize that you need to be changed and then take the steps necessary to rewire your brain. You could view this learning as a cycle to make it easier.

There are three things you can do to help create a growth mindset:

- You have to realize that having a growth mindset isn't just good; it is supported by science. This is saying that you have to be committed to creating a growth mindset.

- You can learn and then teach other people about the ways to improve and develop their abilities by adapting to a growth mindset. This can help you have control over your life. This can be very empowering. Science has shown that people who feel like they are in control of their lives usually perform better.

- Listen for a voice that is your fixed mindset. Anytime you hear a little, tiny critical voice in the back of your mind saying: "you can't do that," you can tell it to shut up that you can learn anything you want to.

Using a Growth Mindset Throughout Life

Growth mindsets aren't just to help you learn new things. They can affect how we think about everything in life. A growth mindset could help you do better at work, in relationships, and sports.

Creating a growth mindset might just be the most important thing that you could ever do to help you get everything you want out of life.

Are Certain People Smarter Than Others?

This can be answered with both "no" and "yes." When we are born, we have a genetic structure that is unique to us. This means that we are initially better than some people at various things. But, people who have developed a growth mindset believe that they can always catch up, improve, and move passed another's innate talents. This is the part where teachers help shape their student's outlook and confidence by giving them continuous, productive feedback. It is critical for teachers who understand the growth mindset do everything in their power to unlock that learning.

Can We Share Mindsets?

Sure. Humans can operate in both growth and fixed mindset. You might be wondering how we can operate in both growth and fixed mindset. Look at this example: Many people have a mindset that is fixed about jumping off a cliff. You hold no beliefs in being able to fly. You know you can't practice jumping off of a table or chair to be able to fly. Knowing you can't fly and you can't practice learning how to fly is an appropriate, normal fixed mindset.

When a person has a fixed mindset, they believe in their natural talent or intelligence as just fixed. They take time to document their talent or intelligence rather than developing them further. They believe that their talents are all they need to reach success. They don't think they need to put any additional effort into it.

If a person has a growth mindset, they think that they can develop their abilities with hard work and practice. Their talents and brains are just the beginning. By having this view, they can learn to love learning new things and have a resilience that is needed for great accomplishments.

Having a growth mindset is simply believing that you can develop your abilities and improve them through hard work and dedication. It isn't so much that these beliefs are magical. It is more the fact that without having a growth mindset, you won't exert the needed effort and you will stay stuck where you are at.

With a growth mindset, you can break through the "stickiness" and reach all the results that you desire. This might be moving up the corporate ladder, finding the love of your life, renewing your relationship with your partner, or any other aspect in your life.

Having a growth or fixed mindset can impact a student's learning experience from elementary school and into high school. Students who have a fixed mindset will give up if they can't figure out a problem. They will just admit defeat. This can damage their efforts in the future and could lead to limited growth. If they have a growth mindset, they will continuously try to improve their skills, and this can lead to more growth and then success.

How to Know If You Have A Growth Mindset

Do you think you were born with a particular set of abilities and skills, and these skills will stay with you for your whole life? For example, your IQ.

Do you believe any of the following about yourself?:

"It's hard for me to lose weight."
"I'm not good with numbers."
"I'm not an athlete."
"I'm not creative."
"I'm a procrastinator."

If you answered "yes," you have a fixed mindset, which will likely lead you to avoid experiences where you might feel like a failure.

Do you think that your beliefs and ideas are

always changing, and you can learn new skills if you try, and your intelligence and wisdom can grow with every unique experience?

If you answered "yes," you have a growth mindset.

It is okay if you have a fixed mindset. You can create a growth mindset. We will go over more about how to build it below.

Why Does It Matter?

The way we encourage and interact with our children can affect their attitude toward learning. Having a positive mindset makes the difference between a person giving up just because they aren't good at spelling and a determined struggle that brings growth. Having a growth mindset isn't all about effort. If a person has a fixed mindset, all they think about is the outcome. If they fail or they weren't the best, their effort was just wasted. For a person with a growth mindset, they value everything they do, no matter what the outcome. They tackle their problems, chart new courses, and work on important issues. They might not have found a cure for cancer, but they are still searching.

If you have a fixed mindset, you might shy away from challenges because you don't want to feel humiliated and embarrassed. Nobody does. This could be a problem due to a fear of making mistakes that could cause you to stay away from new experiences and challenges that might help you grow, improve yourself, and create a life you have always wanted.

If you have a growth mindset, you embrace

facing challenges despite all the risks. This happens because you love growing and learning more than letting other people think you know what you are doing. Since you are always trying new things, you usually don't know exactly what you are doing. But those people who have a growth mindset usually build new skills easier because you believe you can, and you work hard at it.

Creating a growth mindset can help you have a fuller, more meaningful life since your life experiences will be a lot broader.

Main Differences Between Growth and Fixed Mindsets

- Feedback and Mistakes

A person with a fixed mindset hates to make a mistake because they feel embarrassed. They might blame someone else or get defensive when criticized. A person with a growth mindset will view mistakes as a lesson they can learn from and won't take the criticism personally. When you are open to criticism, it can help you improve your ability to do better. This is just one more reason why having a growth mindset could bring you to success.

- Challenge

A person with a fixed mindset will stay away from challenges because they are afraid of failing and might hide just to avoid your responsibilities. A person with a growth mindset will find challenges engaging and exciting because they know they are going to learn valuable things from experience. They stay with the challenge, master it, and then they move on to bigger accomplishments.

- Effort

If a person with a fixed mindset is met with hard work, they might recruit other people to do the hard work or find an excuse to avoid it. They won't spend any effort to do what needs to be done. If a person with a growth mindset is met with hard work, they recognize that great accomplishments will require effort and persistence. Effort is a vital part of this process. If they want to master something new, they will have to apply a lot of energy, whether it be physical, mental, or repeating something over and over.

Ways to Build Your Growth Mindset

Changing your mindset from being fixed to growth might seem hard to do, but if you take baby steps, if you want it bad enough, you can create a growth mindset.

Here is how you can do it:

- Realize and Embrace Your Imperfections

You need to be able to see and embrace all the imperfections in yourself and in others since it is the spice that makes us all unique. Everyone has flaws, deficiencies, and peculiarities. Just like the mole on Marilyn Monroe's face, imperfections make everyone unique.

- Bravely Face Your Challenges

If you realize that you are scared when faced with a challenge, stop and reframe the challenge in your mind. Think about your challenges as opportunities; by shifting your perspective just a bit, you will make it easier to engage with the challenge. Every challenge is an opportunity that is inviting us to experience new adventures.

Try various approaches to help coach yourself about ways to explore new paths or ways to create new skills, or ways to interact with new people, or ways to get through new circumstances. Fear is a feeling that we all can accept. You keep moving forward because it is new and exciting. If you can take this same attitude with a new challenge or a crisis at work, you might find new abilities that you never knew you possessed.

- Watch Your Thoughts and Words

Begin paying attention to what you say, even what you say in your mind. If your words are dark or low, it can cause the same results. You have to watch yourself; listen to everything you think and say. Begin censoring yourself and be your own guide.

You have to replace all negative thoughts with positive ones to create a growth mindset. Replace judgments with acceptance, hate with compassion, and doubt with confidence. If you disrespect yourself or lower your ethics, the outcome of these decisions and the consequences are going to reflect that. Have an intention to think better thoughts and keep yourself accountable.

- Quit Looking for Approval

When you look for approval from other people, it can keep us from developing a growth mindset. You have to cultivate your self-approval and self-acceptance. You have to learn how to trust yourself. You are the only one who is always going to be there for you your whole life, so ultimately, you are the only person you should be trying to impress.

- Become More Authentic

When you pretend to be a person who you aren't will disrespect the true you. It shows that you are a fake. It lessens all that you have to offer. Becoming authentic is a process that is going to take a lot of time and work. When you do, you will be more driven to go after your goals, and this puts you in a growth mindset.

- Have a Sense of Purpose

Do you feel like you have a purpose in life? If you do, figure out what this purpose holds. If you just draw a blank, ask yourself what your life's purpose is until it gets clear. Think about or meditate on what your purpose may be. Sit for a few minutes until you get a clear picture of what your life purpose is. Once you know what it is, make up your mind to pursue it. That will help you create your growth mindset.

- Rethink the Word Genius

Everyone has weaknesses and strengths. Identify and then appreciate your strengths and work on improving your weaknesses.

- Find Criticism's Gifts

The goal of constructive criticism is to coach and provide feedback. Other people can see what you are doing from a different perspective and might have some suggestions for you that can help you improve. It can be challenging to receive criticism from a co-worker, a peer, or someone that you don't fully respect, but it's important to remember that accurate and constructive feedback comes even from flawed sources. If you are open to hearing these suggestions and do not get defensive, you give yourself an opportunity for development and growth.

- The Process is Valuable

You need to value the process more than the result. It is the journey that matters and not the destination.

- Learn from Other People's Mistakes

If you have the ability the learn from other people's mistakes; you might be able to make fewer mistakes. This might lessen the fear when you are trying new things. This is the central aspect of creating your growth mindset.

- It is Okay to Say "Not Yet"

If you are struggling with something, remind yourself that it is okay; you just haven't mastered it "yet." If you just stick with it, practice and time are going to lead to improvement.

- Take Risks When You're with Others

Stop taking yourself so seriously. You need to be willing to make some mistakes in front of other people. If you are still growing, this is going to happen. The more often you embarrass yourself in front of others, the less it will bother you.

- Set Realistic Timelines

Acknowledge that it is going to take some time. It will take time to learn a new skill, such as playing an instrument or a new language. You might want to become a lawyer which is going to take a lot of time. Remember that being realistic can help you with your growth mindset.

- Speed Isn't Important

If you have a growth mindset, your end results won't matter. You will completely engage and put in all the effort that it is going to take, and it won't matter how long it takes you to get the results. When you focus on the process, it will usually improve the results since you put in a lot of effort on the way.

- It's Your Attitude, Own It

If you want to have a growth mindset, you have to take the time and make an effort to create it. If you persist, opportunities will come your way.

You will be pursuing resilience on your way. You are remolding your mind, and that is a great thing.

<u>Recap</u>

When you have a growth mindset, it means that you are embracing challenges, persisting when you face any setbacks, taking responsibility for your actions and words, and acknowledging all the effort on the path toward success. This is the reason why "practice makes perfect."

When you choose to take extra efforts to create your growth mindset, you will be able to make all your mental processes work for you. This can result in a large possibility that you will get the results that you are looking for and you will be able to live the life that you want.

Positive Mindset Mastery

Chapter 4: Understanding Negativity

We all engage in negative thinking now and then, but constant negativity will destroy your mental health, causing you to feel anxious and depressed. Science has found that positive thinking can improve our mental wellbeing, lower our stress levels, and lead to better cardiovascular health. Yet, most of us get stuck in negative thought patterns. Let's explore the world of negative thinking.

What Counts as a Negative Thought?

If you analyze your thoughts, it can be difficult to differentiate negative thinking from simple worries that everybody has. Feeling sad about something that is upsetting is normal, just like it's normal to worry about relationship troubles or financial burdens. But it is when those feelings become pervasive and repetitive that problems show up.

Negative thinking is when you have a negative view of yourself and your surroundings. While most people will experience negative thoughts, negative thinking that seriously affects the way you view yourself and the world around, and even interferes with your life, could be a sign of mental illness.

Not everybody who experiences negative thinking will have a mental illness, just like not everybody who has a mental illness suffers from constant negative thoughts. That said, negative thinking can seriously hurt your quality of life and mental health, especially if you aren't able to stop it. Luckily, there are ways to bring those thoughts to an end, but you have first to know what causes them.

<u>Negativity Bias</u>

We've all been there when we catch ourselves dwelling on a mistake. Criticism tends to affect us a lot more than compliments, and bad news always gets more attention. The reason this happens is negative events simply have a more significant impact than positive ones. This is what psychologists call a negativity bias. This bias can have a massive effect on our actions, decisions, and relationships.

Negativity bias is our tendency to register

negative things more often than we do positive things, as well as to dwell on those things. This causes us to feel the pain of rejection more than we would feel the joy of praise (Maloney, 2020).

This is the reason why bad first impressions can be so hard to overcome and why our previous traumas can linger for so long. In pretty much every interaction we have, there's a greater chance of noticing negative things and remembering them more vividly later on.

We all tend to:

- Respond strongly to negative events.
- Remember negative things more often than positive ones.
- React in a strong way to negative stimuli.
- Recall the insults we have received rather than praise.

- Remember our traumatic experiences more vividly.

For example, you could be having an amazing time at a family get-together when one of your relatives makes an offhand comment that irritates you. You start to notice that you are stewing over what they said for the rest of the party. Once you get home, and somebody mentions the party, you reply about how horrible it was, even though, for the most part, it was a good party.

Research has found that this negative bias will also influence our motivation to finish a task. People are more motivated if something they desire is going to be taken away as opposed if the incentive is to give them something.

This can play a significant role in your

motivation to reach your goals. Instead of focusing on the things that you are going to gain, you may want to focus on what you are going to lose if you don't reach that goal.

Other studies have also found that people assume that negative news is always the truth. Since negative information will draw people's attention more, it can be seen as having more validity. This is likely why bad news tends to get more attention.

This negative tendency is likely due to an evolutionary process. Earlier in human history, noticing dangerous, harmful, or negative threats in the world was a matter of life and death. Those who paid more attention to danger were more likely to live. This means that they were also more likely to hand down the genes that made them more attentive to danger.

Neuroscience has found that there is more neural processing within the brain when it comes to negative stimuli. Psychologist John Cacioppo conducted studies where he showed participants pictures that were either neutral, positive, or negative and observed the electrical activity within their brain. He found that there was a stronger response within the cerebral cortex when they saw negative images than when they viewed neutral or positive ones (Maloney, 2020).

What Causes Negative Thoughts?

There are many different causes of negative thinking. Intrusive negative thoughts may be a sign of generalized anxiety disorder, OCD, depression, or some other mental health condition. While negative thoughts can signal a possible mental health problem, it can also simply be a part of life and your internal programming. Since these negative thoughts can affect you so much, you should learn what is causing them.

There are three leading causes of negative thoughts.

1. Fear of the Future

People tend to fear the unknown and don't know what the future may hold. This can cause a person to start catastrophizing, which means they think the future is going to be a disaster. Whichever way you see it, worrying about what the future holds is just a waste of energy. The key to releasing these negative thoughts is to accept that you cannot predict the future, and it's more rewarding to focus on the present.

2. Anxiety about the Present

It's understandable to be anxious about the present. Many of us worry about how others feel about us, if we are doing well at work, and how long we will be stuck in traffic during our commute. Negative thinking, on the other hand, will come up with the worst-case scenario. They think nobody at work likes them, and the boss is about to tell them they are the worst employee, which is going to make them late to pick up their kids from school. Again, all of this comes from the fear of losing control. Routine and organization can help get rid of some of these negative thoughts, but you might also find help through practical therapy techniques.

3. Shame about the Past

Have you ever laid awake in bed worrying about

something you did yesterday, last week, or last year? Everyone has had disappointing moments at some point, but negative thinkers will often dwell on past failures and mistakes much more than other people will. Of course, a better approach would be to accept that they happened and think about how you could prevent it from occurring again in the future.

Why Can't They Just Stop?

For anybody who suffers from intrusive negative thoughts, hearing somebody say, "Why can't you just be happy" makes you feel hopeless, angry, or any other negative emotion. The thing is, you want to feel happier. Nobody wants to be stuck in those negative thoughts, but they are hard to stop. It's important to point out - if you do suffer from negative thoughts, it does not make you a bad person, no matter what other people may say to you.

There is a reason why these negative thoughts are hard to get rid of. Negative thoughts are like a train wreck; you don't want to look, but you just can't look away. While it may be dreadful to see, it is also exhilarating.

This enticement happens when the brain releases reward chemicals, like dopamine. Since we receive a reward for those thoughts, they get repeated over and over again until they become habitual. Within the brain, we form these habits in the basal ganglia, which is the oldest and most primitive part of our brain. This is what scientists call the "lizard brain."

Since we form habits in such a primitive area of the brain, they pretty much get hardwired in. They have such deep roots in our brain; some scientists believe that habits can't be destroyed and can only be replaced by new ones. For example, a person may smoke to have a break from their workday. When you feel bored, you choose to go outside a chew a piece of gum instead. When you do this enough times, the habit of smoking will be replaced with the habit of chewing gum.

The issue here is that negative thoughts aren't just a habit. When the brain believes that some bad is also beneficial, it turns into an addiction. In most cases, when a person replaces an addiction, it gets replaced with something that's equally, if not more, dangerous, like drugs or drinking. While this sounds very hopeless, there is hope; continue reading.

Types of Negativity

Negative thoughts and negativity can show up in many different ways, most of which you will likely be familiar with.

1. Cynicism

This is where a person has a general distrust of people and their motives.

2. Hostility

This is where a person is unfriendly to others, and they are unwilling to create a healthy relationship.

3. Filtering

This is where a person notices only the bad in what should be a happy moment.

4. Polarized Thinking

This is a belief that if someone or something isn't perfect, then it has to be horrible.

5. Jumping to Conclusions

This is where a person assumes something terrible is going to happen because of their present circumstances.

6. Catastrophizing

This is the belief that disaster is inevitable.

7. Blaming

This is where a person blames others for personal problems and feel as if they are the victim of the uncontrollable events of life.

8. Emotional Reasoning

This is where a person uses their emotions to define what is real and what isn't.

9. Fallacy of Change

This is a thought process where if a person or circumstance changes, you will then be happy.

10. Heaven's Reward Fallacy

This is a type of negativity where a person assumes that there is always going to be a reward for sacrifice and hard work. When they don't get the reward, they become depressed and bitter.

The Dangers of Negative Thoughts

Once your negative thoughts move from normal, given the circumstances, into intrusive and constant, you are opening yourself up to many dangers. Constant negative thoughts can cause mood disorders, high blood pressure, depression, and chronic anxiety.

Physically, negativity can show up in the form of:

- Drastic metabolism changes
- Sleep problems
- Upset stomach
- Fatigue
- Chest pains
- Headache

Mentally, negativity can show up in the form of:

- Social withdrawal
- Depression
- Anxiety
- Schizophrenia
- Personality disorders

The reason why constant negative thoughts can have such a negative effect on not just your mind but your body as well is that it causes chronic stress. This stress upsets your hormonal balance, damages the immunes system, and depletes the brain of chemicals needed for happiness. Chronic stress can decrease lifespan.

For example, hostility, or anger, if poorly managed or repressed, can cause a slew of health problems, like high blood pressure, infections, digestive disorders, and cardiovascular disease.

Let's look at what cynicism can do. A 2014 study by the American Academy of Neurology connected high levels of cynicism later in life to a higher risk of dementia when compared to those who were more trusting. This was even after taking into account other risk factors like smoking, certain heart health markers, sex, and age.

Our emotions and thoughts have widespread effects on how our body works, such as immune function, hormone release, and metabolism. Plus, there is the fact that when somebody is feeling down, they are more likely to take part in drinking or smoking or other unhealthy habits.

<u>Negativity in Relationships</u>

Beyond just the personal effects of negativity, it can affect your relationships as well, especially those of the romantic kind. We know how a negativity bias causes us to focus on the bad, more so than the good. Well, think about how that works in a relationship. Negativity holds up a magnifying glass to your partner's faults, whether real or imagined. You are also biased by your own confidence that magnifies your strengths. You start to wonder how your partner could possibly be so selfish and blind to all of your virtues and everything you have done for them. You start asking, why don't they appreciate me?

Psychologists have found, by asking couples to rate their satisfaction in the relationship, that things typically decline over time. They also found that the most successful marriages are defined not by improvement, but by avoiding that decline. This doesn't mean marriage is hopeless, but that initial thrill of infatuation is going to fade, and that's why couples have to find other sources of contentment. But there are times when this decline in satisfaction is so steep that it dooms the marriage.

Let's look at a scenario. Your partner does something that annoys you. It could be anything from spending too much, ignoring you while you talk, or flirting with your friends. How will you respond?

1. Let it go and hope it gets better.

2. Explain what is bothering you and work out a compromise.

3. Sulk. Don't speak up, but emotionally pull away from them.

4. Head for the door. Threaten to leave them or start looking for someone new.

In one study, psychologists identified two basic strategies that couples use when faced with these types of problems, constructive and destructive. Each of these strategies could be active or passive.

The constructive strategies were admirable and didn't make much of a difference in the relationship long-term. Remaining passively loyal, as in the first response, didn't have a significant impact on the relationship, and actively trying to reach a solution, as in the second response, only helped things a little.

What was more intriguing was the results of the destructive strategies. If you start to withdraw silently, as in the third response, or you get angry and throw around threats, as in the fourth, you can create a disastrous spiral of retaliation. When this happens, it creates a significant strain on the relationship. The negativity has taken over, and it's hard to overcome it. That's why it is so important to learn how to identify and control your negative bias, so it isn't able to take hold of your life or your relationships.

Working Through Three Common Negative Thinking Patterns

It can be difficult to identify negative thinking patterns, mainly because our thoughts feel so true. We tend to accept them uncritically and don't question them. We are going to look at three common negative thought patterns and how you can change them to something healthier.

1. Negative Rumination

While this natural and can be a healthy way to self-reflect, reflection ends up becoming a problem when it is repetitive, negative, and excessive. Rumination is a negative thinking pattern where you get mentally stuck and continue to spin your wheels without moving forward at all, like a car stuck in the mud. Rumination can end up making you feel more anxious as you continue to stew on the negative outcomes that may happen.

When you notice yourself ruminating, do something to change your thoughts up. Try taking a walking or talking to a friend. Make sure, though, if you choose to talk, don't start talking about what you were ruminating over.

2. Overthinking

Overthinking happens when you start to process different options over and over, trying to figure out all possible outcomes and everything that might occur in the future, to make sure you make the best choice. The problem with this is that you attempt to try to control something that you can't control. There is no way to predict the future. With every choice, there is going to be an unknown.

What you should do is limit the time you spend thinking about the decisions you need to make before acting. Make a deadline as to when the decision needs to be made, even if it doesn't feel comfortable. Only give yourself the chance to research a few alternative options, not every single one.

3. Cynical Hostility

This is a way of thinking and reacting that is marked by angry mistrust of others. You view people as threats. You think that they may deceive you, let you down, take advantage of you, cheat on you, or otherwise cause you harm. Cynical hostility means you interpret other people's behavior in the worst way. You may believe that a driver in front of you is deliberately driving slow to make you mad or that your friends have some ulterior motive.

What you should do instead is try to get a bit of distance between you and the judging thoughts. Notice when you start to think in a distrustful way, and deliberately think of other ways to view the situations. What is something that could be motivating a person's actions that are benevolent or less toxic? Learn to reserve your judgments and look for actual evidence before you label a person. Notice how your own actions can push people away or prompt them to react negatively towards you.

Other Ways to Overcome Negativity

Negative thoughts can appear in many different ways, so it's important to be prepared for any negative thoughts that may arise. We will finish out this chapter by looking at some other ways to train yourself to stop having so many negative thoughts.

1. Schedule Your Negative Thoughts

This may seem paradoxical, but you can gain control over your negative thoughts by scheduling ten minutes a day to ruminate and review those negative thoughts. If you experience a negative thought during the day, write it down, and tell yourself that you will review it during your NTT (Negative Thought Time). The NTT has to be every day and can only last ten minutes. Over time, you will start to gain control over your negative thoughts.

2. Replacing the Negative Thought

Getting rid of the negative thoughts usually is easier to do if you simply replace it with a positive thought. This can be done in four steps. First, notice when you start the pattern. Second, acknowledge that it is a pattern you want to get rid of. Three, articulate what you would like to do differently. Four, choose a different behavior that is going to serve your goal.

3. Write It Down

Write down the reason for your negative thoughts. Writing things down, versus thinking about them, helps to purge the thought, and when you see it on paper, it makes it easier to understand it.

4. Ask Tough Questions

Take some time to reflect on your answers to these questions:

- What do these negative thought patterns give you?
- What do I lose when I engage in these negative thoughts?

- What benefits would I have if I engaged in positive thoughts?
- What happened in my past that has caused me to be negative?
- What will I do now?

5. Give Up the Morning News

Research has found that only three minutes of negative news in the morning will increase the odds of a negative experience during the day. Research has also found that a positive mindset can increase satisfaction and productivity.

Recap

Negative thinking can't be avoided altogether, but it can be controlled. Allowing your negative thoughts to become compulsive and uncontrollable, you are risking the damaging side effects of these thoughts. Start taking note of the times that you think negatively, and then learn how to keep them at bay. Schedule your negative time so that it doesn't consume your entire day.

Positive Mindset Mastery

Chapter 5: Understanding Anger

What exactly is anger? It is one of our basic emotions. It is just as elemental as disgust, anxiety, sadness, or happiness. All of our emotions are tied to our survival, and we have been honed throughout history. Anger is a close relative to the freeze, flight, or fight response. It gets us ready to fight. Fighting doesn't have to mean hitting someone; it may motivate a community to take on some form of injustice by enforcing new behaviors or changing a law or two.

If you get angry too often or too easily, it can harm your relationships, and it could be harmful to your body. Having too many stress hormones released into the body can destroy neurons in the brain that is associated with short-term memory and judgment. It can also weaken your immune system.

How to Control Anger

Everybody has felt that feeling. It's the rage that comes up when someone cuts you off on the road. You just want to push the gas pedal to the floor and make an obscene gesture to them. Anger won't go away just because you express it. This can actually deepen and reinforce it.

Just like any other emotion, anger needs to be driven through self-awareness, so it won't erupt into violent, aggressive, or hostile behaviors toward other people or causes you to harm yourself. Most cities have support groups that help you manage your anger. These can either be in individual or group settings. Cognitive restructuring might also help because they help the patient to reframe their inflammatory and unhealthy thoughts.

When Does Anger Become a Disorder?

Everybody is going to feel angry at some point in their lives. It becomes a problem when the severity or frequency of your anger interferes with your mental health, legal standing, performance at work, or relationships. Even though there isn't an official "anger disorder," dysfunctional anger is a symptom of manic episodes, "intermittent explosive disorder," and "borderline personality disorder." You don't need a formal diagnosis for anger to get disruptive or to get help managing it.

What Causes Anger

There are nine main reasons anger can occur:

1. Unmet Needs or A Threat to Safety

Maslow came up with a hierarchy of needs. These are things that a person requires to feel safe and happy in their life. Before anybody can deal with the needs high up on the pyramid, their basic needs have to be met. These basic needs include food, water, warmth, rest, security, and safety. When those basic needs aren't satisfied, we can experience anger.

This anger results from the fact that we have to start fighting for those needs. The longer the deprivation lasts, the more motivated we are to fulfill those needs. For example, the longer a person is without food, the hungrier they become. We become willing to fight for these needs to be met. If these needs aren't satisfied, then our body is unable to function optimally.

2. Grief and Loss

When we lose someone that we were close to, we go through five stages of grief. This includes denial, anger, bargaining, depression, and acceptance. To move to the next stage, you have to work through the present, but why do we get angry?

Becoming angry during grief is connected to the previous cause of anger. Our basic human needs are threatened. Then you add in the other changes that happen after the death of a loved one. It could cause a change of location, financial status, family relations, and more. This anger can show up in many different ways. You could be angry at the love who died. You could be angry with your higher power for taking your loved one. You could be angry at the disease that took them. Often, it is easier to express anger than try to figure out why we are really upset.

3. Boundaries are Violated

Healthy individuals have boundaries. Boundaries protect us from being taken advantage of or being run too thin. They are beneficial to have, and all individuals should create boundaries. That said, sometimes those boundaries get violated. When that happens, we may respond with anger. Anger is pretty intense, so chances are if you do get angry at a person for your boundary violation, then they have likely been ignoring your boundaries for a while.

In a sense, when they ignore your boundaries, they are disrespecting you, telling you that your feelings don't matter and that they are trying to control you. This is why we end up angry at those people.

4. Disappointment and Shattered Expectations

We hate to be disappointed, whether in ourselves or others. To feel disappointed means that something has let you down. Things didn't go as planned, or a person didn't act as you had hoped they would. When something always disappoints you, it can end up causing you to feel angry. This ties back into the first point of our basic needs, especially if it has to do with a person in our life that we see as a parental figure. We are supposed to be able to rely on them, but if we can't, we think we have lost our security. Thus, feelings of disappointment and anger arise.

5. Guilt and Shame-Based Identity

Anger can be used to cover up guilt and shame. This is because we react defensively when we get criticized or even get mild feedback. This means we use anger to divert attention away from the pain.

6. Unforgiveness – Bitterness, Resentment, and Revenge

Bitterness, resentment, and revenge are low-grade anger responses. A perception of unfairness triggers these emotions. If somebody didn't praise you when you thought they should, you might feel resentful. The problem is, we often stick with these emotions.

We don't forgive the person we believe wronged us, and this low-grade anger response starts to build into full-blown anger. Sometimes by the time, it reaches ahead, we have forgotten what caused us to get upset in the first place.

7. Vitamin Deficiency

While this may sound weird, a deficiency in B vitamins can be an underlying cause of anger. B vitamins are connected to preserving brain health. B1 and B5 specifically lead to symptoms of irritability. Having a B vitamin deficiency is often caused by a lack of micronutrients in your diet.

8. Substance Abuse

Substance abuse and anger are two sides of a

coin. Often, a person will have anger before they start abusing drugs or alcohol. They get so consumed in their rage; they are willing to try anything to put an end to it, so they turn to substances to try and numb the anger. The problem here is, the substance typically causes feelings of anger to become stronger and harder to control.

9. Unresolved Childhood Distress

Unresolved childhood trauma can cause many different issues in adulthood. One of which is anger. If you grew up in a household where anger was expressed in an unhealthy manner, you might think anger is bad. That means you start to suppress the anger because you don't know how to use it correctly. The problem is, you are still angry, but that anger continues to build until it comes out in an unhealthy way.

Everybody Has Triggers

There are several ways our brains can get triggered. These triggers will be different for everybody based on their life experiences. For example, if you were bullied a lot when you were younger, your triggers are going to be very intense towards a person who is threatening or controlling.

Here are some of the most common anger triggers:

- Certain people or personalities
- Not having enough control
- Being disappointed constantly
- Disputes within a relationship
- Lying
- Misinformation
- Insults
- Physical threats

- Blaming
- Shaming
- Labeling
- Abusive language
- Violating your personal space
- Disrespect
- Injustice

Any of these triggers can cause somebody to experience a total amygdala breakdown. Adults who had volatile experiences during childhood could get extremely angry if those situations get recreated in their adult lives.

We have to know what triggers our anger and to be aware of the problems that put our brains on high alert and might send us over the edge. When we have found our triggers, it will help us to determine why they cause this kind of response.

It can be helpful to write down your triggers as you start to recognize them. By doing this, you will prepare yourself for an outburst.

<u>Anticipating Your Anger</u>

Knowing the reasons for your triggers will help you anticipate an outburst. When you know your triggers, you will be able to take control of your anger. You will be keeping the process inside the cortex rather than in the limbic system. You will be able to give a deliberate response that will quiet the outburst.

If you are aware and in tune with your triggers, then you will be able to predict your response and make a choice not to respond angrily. This means that you will be:

- Able to see what is happening around you that caused the trigger, and

- Take any measure necessary to talk yourself into a better response that allows you to handle the way you are reacting.

When you are in charge of your reactions, this comes from maintaining self-control because you know what is happening within your brain, and you know your triggers. Your emotions and thoughts stay in your cortex, where you will be able to be less emotional and more strategic.

<u>Tips to Help You Control Your Anger</u>

Controlling your anger is essential to help you stay away from doing or saying something that you might regret. Before your anger gets out of control, you can use some of the following strategies to help you control it:

- Get Creative

Turn anger into a project. Think about writing a poem, work in the garden, or pain when you get upset. Emotions can be a delightful muse for creative people. Use it to help lessen your anger.

- Express It

It is OK to express the way you feel if you handle it correctly. Ask a friend that you trust to help you be accountable. Outbursts won't solve anything, but talking maturely could help you not feel as angry or stressed. It could prevent problems in your future.

- Have Empathy

Try walking in someone else's shoes and look at the situation from their perspective. If you can relive the events or tell the story from their point of view, you might gain a better understanding and be less angry.

- Write the Person

Write an email or letter to whoever made you feel angry. DON'T send it. Delete it. Most of the time, just expressing your emotions in some way is all you need, even if it is something that won't be seen by anyone other than you.

- Laugh

Nothing can get rid of a bad mood, like getting into a good one. Get rid of your anger by finding ways to laugh. It might be scrolling through some memes, watching your favorite comedian, or playing with your children.

- Change Up Your Routine

If just thinking about your commute to work gets you angry before you have had your morning coffee, try to find a new route to work. Think about options that might take more time but won't leave you frustrated and upset.

- Pause and Go Over Your Response

You can stop an outburst by first pausing for a moment and going over what you will say or the way you were going to approach the problem. This time will give you all the time you need to play out several solutions.

- Find an Immediate Solution

You may be angry that your child left their toys thrown all over their room before they went to a friend's house. Close their door. You can put a temporary end to your anger just by getting it out of your sight. Look for similar resolutions for all other situations, no matter how subtle it may seem.

- Journal About It

All the things that you can't say to a person, maybe you can write about it. Write down all the things you are feeling and ways you would like to respond to them. Processing them through writing could help you calm down and look at the events that brought you to what you are feeling in this present moment.

- Take Some Action

You can harness your angry energy by doing something productive. Write a letter to your congressman, mayor, or whomever about some law that needs to be changed. Do something nice for somebody who lives close to you. If you have elderly neighbors, check and see if they need any help. Pour all those emotions and energy into something productive and healthy.

- Give Yourself a Time Out

Take a break. Sit by yourself. During this quiet time, you will be able to process all the events and get your emotions back to normal. You might even realize that this time by yourself is very helpful, and you want to do this on a daily basis.

- Listen to Music

I've always heard the old saying of: "Music calms the savage beast." Allow the music to carry you far away from what you are feeling. Go to your car or put on some headphones.

Tune into your favorite music and dance, bop, hum, or sing your anger away.

- Escape Mentally

Find a quiet place, close your eyes, and just imagine yourself relaxing in your favorite vacation spot. Notice every detail of this imaginary place: What is around you? Do you hear water running? Are you on a sandy beach? Is there a breeze blowing? This can help you find peace in the middle of anger.

- Go for a Walk

Exercise has been known to help reduce anger and calm the nerves. Take a walk, ride your bike, or hit the gym. Anything that gets you moving and your heart pumping is good for the body and mind.

- Count

It doesn't matter which way you count. It can be up or down in increments of ten. If you are outraged, begin at 100 or go to 100. In the time it takes you to count, your heart rate will slow down, and your anger will disappear.

Suppressing Your Emotions

It isn't just long-term health that might suffer if you continuously suppress your emotions. There have been many studies that have shown when we ignore or mismanage our emotions, it can create short-term physical and mental deficiencies.

When you suppress your emotions, whether it is frustration, grief, sadness, or anger, it could cause lots of physical stress on the body. The effects will be the same, even if the emotions are different. It could affect your self-esteem, memory, and blood pressure.

If you suppress your emotions for a long time, you have a more considerable risk of heart disease and diabetes. Neglecting your emotions could lead to problems with depression, anxiety, aggression, and memory.

When you don't acknowledge your emotions, you are just making them stronger. For example, you may be angry at your sister, and after you have sat and stewed in this anger, but still didn't say anything, you are encouraging an outburst.

A few weeks have passed, and you are going to work, a car cuts you off, you immediately go into full-blown road rage and hit them, causing a huge accident. That overreaction and explosion of emotions to this situation was your body's way of releasing all those pent-up emotions.

Handling Strong Emotions

Learning the right way to handle your emotions is hard. There are some steps you can take if you are feeling overly emotional and don't know how to handle it.

- Take Time to Take Care of Yourself

Any kind of activity that allows you to take care of yourself, relaxes you, or calms you down can be beneficial. Studies show that exercise can help with emotional stress. If you are experiencing some challenging emotions, you can regulate them by doing meditation, some aerobic exercises, or you could practice gratitude and forgiveness toward the person or situation.

- Own Your Response

To know what you are feeling, you need to think about the way you dealt and reacted to the situation. Take some time to really think about what got you to where you are at. Now think about ways you can keep that from happening in the future. If it is something that can't be avoided, like grief, think about it and ways you can handle it better using some of the tips provided previously.

- Confront It

If you can, confront the situation or person that is triggering your emotion with a goal in mind of resolving that problem. If you can't do this, learn how to "observe" the situation to empower yourself.

When you "observe," you are taking yourself out of the problem and not taking the situation personally. Look at the situation as if you aren't a part of it. Calmly figure out what the other person was feeling or thinking and what could have made them act a specific way.

When you observe a situation, it allows you to learn more about a person instead of getting frustrated, angry, or taking their actions personally. If you can't confront the problem, talking to someone you trust can lessen the emotion and could have therapeutic effects on your brain.

- Acknowledge Your Emotions

Realizing that you are feeling a certain way is

very important. You don't need to do this out loud; you can do this internally. You might think you are feeling angry, but it might be something more complex. You might be feeling sad, but you revert to anger because it is an emotion you are more comfortable with.

You need to find and understand the core emotion behind your feelings. Take the time to answer these questions:

- "Why am I feeling this reaction?"

- "Why am I acting this way?"

Just finding and describing the feeling could have beneficial effects.

Recap

Anger is a rational emotion in certain situations. We can't continue to make people suppress their anger just because we are afraid of the emotion. The first thing you need to do is learn your triggers. Once you recognize your triggers, you can start doing what you need to do to express your anger healthily and safely.

Positive Mindset Mastery

Chapter 6: Understanding Pessimism

The clouds in the sky never seen to have a silver lining, and your glass is half empty. Pessimists take a lot of crap because of their negativity and always expecting the worst in everything.

Other than taking a toll on your mental health, your physical health might be hurt, too. Pessimism, even though it might be useful when in moderation or isolation, has been associated with heart disease, high blood pressure, hostility, sleep disorders, depression, and anxiety.

Handling Pessimism

Having expectations that are realistic instead of taking extreme negative or positive positions might be the best recipe for happiness and good health. It might not be surprising but having low levels of pessimism instead of high levels of optimism, have been associated with better health.

This means that pessimism might be one more risk factor for heart disease and other mental and physical health problems; however, being overly optimistic isn't going to prevent you from getting sick. Instead of constantly having a sunny disposition and a bright smile, or giving a negative outlook on life, your goal needs to be moderate optimism with a small dose of pessimism.

Can a Person Catch Pessimism?

Just like other negative feelings, pessimism could be spread from person to person if they spend enough time together. It might be extremely hard for romantic partners or family to stay away from catching cynical outlooks. A few factors that might make someone more susceptible to "catching" pessimism include their stress levels, personal history, genetics, and other factors.

Can Pessimism be a Good Thing?

Pessimists can make better leaders, especially if there is a need to create some social change. Their skepticism might make them resist false advertising and propaganda. Defensive pessimism can be useful as a cognitive strategy for many people. They start by setting their expectations low, and then they outperform themselves by being prepared for multiple negative outcomes.

I don't believe in the idea that we have to be smiling and totally happy every minute of every day. And there may be times when a pessimistic view may be valuable. Pessimism might keep you guarded against making some mistakes. It might give you a full picture of any situation rather than being gullible. However, it's role should be a supporting role and not leading. If you allow it to call all the shots, it is going to say "no" to everything. There isn't anything more limiting than that.

To learn about pessimism, you should know about optimism, too.

What Is Optimism?

"A pessimist sees the difficulty in every opportunity; an optimist sees the opportunity in every difficulty." - Winston Churchill

For psychologists, optimism shows that we believe that the outcome of most experiences or events will be positive. Others believe that optimism is a style; it lives in how people perceive events. Optimists typically see any negative experiences or failures as only temporary and aren't permanent. This type of perspective supports a Growth Mindset, which promotes the development and growth of the individual.

What Does It Mean to Be An Optimist

Optimism doesn't mean you engage in fantastic or wishful thinking. It is a way to look at the world that gives you more influence to change your perspective when life isn't going so great. Optimists will have healthier outlooks, and research has shown that they tend to live longer than pessimists. They aren't as susceptible to depression, fatigue, and illness. However, an unrealistic belief that your future will be full of only positive things could lead them to take some unnecessary risks, especially with their finances and health.

Tips to Help You Think Positively

The best habit you can create is to stop being pessimistic and to think in more constructive ways. It can make you feel lighter. You won't feel burdened down. It can open new paths to all the places you want to go to, and it can help you overcome any setbacks you might have. You won't be as worried all the time. You will stop feeling sorry for yourself. You will feel more motivated to take any actions that are needed.

The benefits of being optimistic are great. How can you create this habit? It will help if you begin to think more positively and stop thinking so skeptically.

Here are ten tips that you can begin using right now to help on your journey:

- Replace the Negative Things in Your Life

All the things that you allow to seep into your mind during your day can have a massive effect on the way you think and feel. You have to begin questioning everything that you allow into your mind. You can do this by asking:

"What are the three biggest negative things in my life?"

It might be someone you see daily at school or work. It might be a website that you visit daily. It could be the music you listen to, a podcast, a television show, or a magazine.

Once you have figured out what these things are, find a piece of paper and ask yourself:

"What can I do to spend less time with these three sources this week?"

Now figure out some ideas and some steps you can do to accomplish this. Now, in the next week, spend the time you have freed up on the positive sources or people that are in your life.

- Find All the Good in Every Negative Situation

The main difference between a pessimist and an optimist is the way that person looks at an obstacle or setback in your life. Anytime I stumbled upon a negative situation, I would just give up and go home. I felt like I was stuck in a permanent place, and it wouldn't matter what I tried. Nothing would make any difference. So my mind would get filled up with pessimistic thoughts, and I would beat myself up for all the things I had done.

I look at things a lot differently now. When I am in a negative situation, I ask myself questions that help to empower me.

Here are some questions you can ask:

- "What is one thing I could do differently the next time to have a better outcome?"
- "What is one thing I could learn from this experience?"

- "What is one good thing about this situation?"
- "How would my parent or best friend help and support me in this situation?"

- Stop Making a Big Deal When There Isn't One

I used to do this all the time. I would blow up the tiniest things into huge monsters. This isn't a great habit if you want to move forward, or you don't want to have a lot of fears or worries in your life.

The easiest way to get yourself grounded in any situation, where you begin to feel like you might be making a big deal out of nothing, is to take a few minutes and ask yourself these questions:

- "Is this going to matter in five minutes?"
- "Is this going to matter if five weeks?"
- "Is this going to matter in five years?"

It might surprise you to know the answer to all of those is, no, it won't.

- Let It Go

If you allow negative things to bounce around in your mind, they will drag you down. To help you let it go, talk about the negative situation with someone you trust. Venting can help you find a better perspective on the situation. While the other person listens to you, you can take the time to figure out what you would like to do.

You might want some more active help. If you both talk about the problem, then you can work together to find a better solution and maybe begin an action plan for all the things you want to make better.

- Take It Slow

If you start going too fast while moving, talking, or even thinking, things won't go too well. Stress can build up, and it will be harder for you to think clearly. Negative thoughts begin to cloud your mind, and it will be hard to stop them. If you can slow your mind, then your body will calm down, too. It will get easier to find an optimistic perspective and constructive ways to get what you want.

- Positively Begin Your Day

The things you do when you wake up can set the tone for your entire day. If you get off to a pessimistic or negative start, then it might be hard to shake these feelings. If you positively start your morning, then it will be a lot easier to remain in that emotional state until it is time to go to bed.

Try placing a reminder on your bathroom mirror or bedside table. It might be a quote that inspires you. It could be something that you are dreaming about getting right now. Write whatever it is on a piece of paper and put it where you will be able to see it in the first few minutes after you get up.

For additional strategies on how to become a more positive thinker, I recommend reading my book Develop a Positive Mindset and Attract the Life of Your Dreams: Unleash Positive

Thinking to Achieve Unbound Happiness, Health, and Success.

Recap

Pessimism causes you to see everything in a negative light, which causes you to feel down all of the time. Start trying to look at things in a more positive and optimistic light. Research has shown that keeping a positive attitude and an optimistic outlook has benefits for your overall health and wellbeing.

Chapter 7: Developing Awareness of Thoughts and Emotions

Tom is a lighting designer at an architecture firm. If you were to ask him if his emotions impact his work, he would laugh in your face. He would tell you that the only thing that matters is being able to turn his client's vision into a design that is aesthetically pleasing and practical. Feelings don't have anything to do with his designs.

Now, ask Tom's coworkers, and you are going to hear a different story. They will tell you that how he works with his coworkers and clients is inconsistent. All will go well when he is in a good mood. His interactions will suffer if he is frustrated or angry. He will show contempt for a suggestion made by a client, plus he won't listen to them. Most of his clients reject his first design because he didn't do what they wanted. His coworkers know that if he is in a bad mood, to stay away from him.

Tom's failure to understand his feelings and the way they can influence his behavior can hurt his work performance. He doesn't have emotional self-awareness.

Emotional Self-Awareness

Emotional self-awareness is being able to understand and recognize emotions and the way they can impact your behavior. You should know the way you feel and why you are feeling like that. You should be able to see how these feelings either hurt or help the things you do. You will also have a good sense of the way others see you. Emotional self-awareness is different from cognitive self-awareness, which focuses on your ideas and thoughts rather than your feelings.

Developing Self-Awareness

Being able to see your feelings and how they influence your actions is a skill that you can develop, just like learning how to play tennis or swim. Just like there are different levels to these skills, noticing feelings isn't something that you do one time and then you have it for the rest of your life. It takes practice and attention to develop. Then you have to maintain by doing it each day, just like practicing mindfulness.

The primary tool for developing your self-awareness is by tuning into your body. If you feel angry or scared, your heart will start pounding faster than when you feel calm. You may start breathing faster and begin sweating. The muscles in your shoulders might tighten up.

Our brains have a map of our bodies. The insula has specific cells that relate to various organs throughout the body. Cell groups in the insula have been tuned into our lungs, heart, and other organs. Interoception is the capacity to sense muscle tension, heart rate, and other signals from the body. The insula will then pass along the signals it gets from our body to the brain. The brain then decides how important the signal is and what it needs to do with this information.

Steps You Can Take to Develop Your Thoughts and Feelings

You know that your thoughts are just an inner dialogue. An average person can have around 6000 thoughts per day, most of these you repeat over and over again. They have essentially become a habit. Many of these thoughts come from the experiences you had from childhood, and you have repeated them ever since.

Why do you need to develop your awareness of these thoughts? Being able to choose the way you think about yourself and your life around you lets you respond, control, and regulate any event that triggers you.

You need to be aware of all the things you tell yourself so you can direct your choices. If you want to be happy, you have to do this. This is crucial since your thoughts can activate processes that are driven by emotions inside you. Yes, even the painful ones. Thoughts, along with your underlying beliefs, can trigger your emotions.

Even though people's actions and events might trigger some unpleasant reactions and feelings, they aren't the cause of them. The activating agents are the things you tell yourself. Most of the things you tell yourself you do on a subconscious level. This comes from all the beliefs that you hold close to you, and most of these operate on a subconscious level.

When you, and not your emotions, are in control of the things you think, you will be in charge of your behavior. This, in turn, gives you more power over the way events will unfold in your life. Developing your self-awareness is the first thing you need to do to start changing your thoughts.

How to Develop Your Emotional Self-Awareness

Here are some steps you can use to help you learn to be aware of your feelings and how they connect to your thoughts.

1. Choose a Situation to Process

Write down a list of events that triggers anger or upsets you. Now choose one that isn't too challenging to work on. With some time and practice, you can take on more and more triggers. You need to work your way up to the more challenging ones gradually. This might take you days, weeks, or even months. You are going to need to be patient. You will have to move out of your comfort zones but don't overwhelm yourself in the process. If at any time, this gets too intense, stop working on this by yourself. If this happens, you might need to find a therapist or counselor who can help you.

1. Ground Yourself in The Present

After choosing the trigger that you want to work on, take a few minutes and take three to five deep breaths, to center yourself. Breathe in deep from the belly and relax your body. Exhale through your mouth and focus. Close your eyes, and focus on your breath, scan your body from your head down to your toes for tension. If you find any, notice it, and then release all tightness and tension.

Visualize yourself inside a safe place. Remember that you aren't your thoughts or emotions. You are the choice maker, creator, and observer of your thoughts and emotions. Remind yourself that this is good. This means you have complete control over how you respond. Nobody can "make you" feel anything without you giving your permission. You are observing your emotions. Notice any emotions that you are experiencing as being old energy pockets. They are old childhood wounds that don't mean anything now. They come from a time when you didn't know how to look at your life from a different perspective. You are now a capable and intelligent adult who is in charge of your mental processes. You get to choose when to stop this exercise. You can stop at any time you need to.

2. Feel and Recognize Your Feelings and Emotions

While you are feeling centered and relaxed with

your breathing, bring the trigger you selected to mind. Try to recall when it happened recently. Don't judge but pause and be aware of your sensations and feelings. If you feel angry, try to find the emotions behind it. These emotions can be a bit overwhelming. You need to ask yourself: "What is lying under this anger?"

What emotions and feelings are you feeling? Jot these down on a piece of paper or in your journal.

3. Notice and Feel Any Sensations

Take a moment and allow yourself to feel every emotion and notice what sensation you feel. For every one of the emotions that got triggered, figure out what sensations you feel when you see the event that triggered this emotion. Notice and observe where these sensations are located. Feel these sensations, breathe into them deeply. Gently place either one or both hands on the place you feel them. While you are doing this, let go of any impulses you have to stop, judge, suppress, or fix these sensations or emotions. Continue exploring and notice if the sensations lessen. If anger is the primary sensation, keep asking yourself: "What else am I feeling?"

Try to describe the sensations you felt in your body. In a column next to the emotions you listed earlier, write down all the sensations you are feeling and where you felt them.

4. Accept Your Feelings

Keep telling yourself that you and your emotions are two different things. You are only observing your emotions. Emotions and energy are the same things. All the things you are feeling are just pockets of supercharged energy that are linked to wounds from your past. Since you are the ruler of your life, you get to choose to breathe into any energy that feels painful, notice if it changes, move, and then release it. You get to decide if you want to affirm the power that you possess as a ruler to accept any painful feelings as being natural due to the circumstance that you are telling yourself. Confidently and calmly affirm: "I accept what I am feeling in this very moment."

Say this either silently or out loud. Out loud would be better: "I can handle this emotion… I am strong and able to handle this calmly, easily, and wisely."

5. Recognize the Things You Tell Yourself That Trigger Painful Emotions

Now, you need to notice the thoughts you think when you visualize the event that triggered your emotions. Try to find any toxic patterns. Your thought can trigger physical sensations and emotions in your body. This is how the brain works.

Observe these thoughts from a distance that is safe and where you are objective. You are just noticing and not judging. Use this visual anytime a disturbing thought comes up. Visualize yourself on a speeding train. You are looking out your window and see all your upsetting thoughts zip by you while you are sitting inside your train car, safe and sound.

Write down anything additional that you tell yourself besides the sensations and emotions that you have already written down.

Recap

Awareness of your emotions and thoughts is 90% of the solution. Once you are away from your emotions, then you can start to heal and form a more positive thought process. Start noticing your emotional triggers and then look at those triggers to see if they are exaggerated or biased from your perception. You will likely find most of your emotional responses to things are somewhat over-the-top. Take advantage of the strategies discussed, and move towards developing a healthy mind and emotionally self-aware.

Chapter 8: Reprogramming Your Mind

Our brains are constantly evolving based on our experiences. Many of us have different beliefs and behaviors now than we did ten years ago. This is due to neuroplasticity. Neuroplasticity is any change in our brain's organization and structure while we learn how to adapt, learn, and experience.

With every repetitive emotion or thought, we are reinforcing a neural pathway. With every new idea, we start creating a new way of living.

These little changes, if repeated enough, can lead to changes in the way our brain works.

The things we do the most get stronger and the things we don't use will eventually fade away. This is the basis of why doing an action or having a thought continuously will increase its power. With time, it will automatically become a part of you. You become what you think and do.

You have to work on rewiring your brain. The brain's connections are getting either weaker or stronger, depending on what you are doing. Younger people find it easier to change because their brains are extremely plastic. However, as we get older, we don't change as quickly. The brain loses some of its plasticity, and we get more fixed in the way we perceive, learn, and think.

Reticular Activating System

The Reticular Activating System (RAS) is a bundle of nerves that sits at our brainstem that can filter out any information that isn't needed, so all the essential things get through. This system is the reason we can learn a new word and then hear it everywhere you go. This is why you can tune out a crowd of people talking but come back to reality when somebody says our name or something similar to it.

The Reticular Activating System sifts through all the data and gives you the critical pieces. This happens without you even realizing it. This system programs itself to work to your advantage without you actually doing anything.

It will look for information that will validate your beliefs. It can filter your world through any parameter you choose to give it. What you believe can shape these parameters. If you think you're bad at talking in front of people, you will be. If you think you work efficiently, you probably will. The RAS can help you see all the things you want to see, and this, in turn, can influence your actions.

There is a belief that you can train your RAS by taking subconscious thoughts and bringing them into your conscious thoughts. This is called "setting your intent." This means if you focus on your goals, your RAS will show you the opportunities, information, and people that can help you reach your goals.

If you set an intention to be more positive and focus on it, you will be more aware and will seek positivity. If you want a pet and you set an intention on getting one, you will find the right information that will lead you to one.

If you focus on bad things, then you are inviting negativity into your life. Focus on all the good things, and they will find you since your brain has been looking for them. It isn't magic; it is your RAS influencing the world as you see it.

Without clear goals, our RAS is similar to a confused personal assistant with no clear instructions from the Boss – you. It will benefit you to create a list of the things you want and read it often. You have to refocus your brain on the things that matter and away from the things that don't.

Emotional Intelligence

Politics, relationships, money, and job pressure; these are just some of the leading causes of stress. This is something that everyone experiences, and it can affect our mental health. We don't have control over all the things that cause us stress, but we can be more aware of our stress indicators and ways we can start managing our stress better. It begins with improving emotional intelligence.

We have heard for years about how we need to see things from other people's perspectives or to have empathy toward others. This can be hard if you aren't aware of your own stressors and ways to regulate yourself. Improving your emotional intelligence can help you handle your stress, empathize with others, building stronger relationships, and reaching your goals. At work, you will be able to assess and change relationships and situations better, cope with stress, demands, and pressures, and negotiate and navigate conflict.

Emotional intelligence can affect the way we relate to others, and this includes the way we lead and manage. If we want to improve our emotional intelligence, we have to know all of its components:

- Self-Awareness

You need to be aware of all the different aspects of yourself, and this includes your feelings and emotions. A self-aware person will be able to understand their emotions while not allowing their feelings to control them. They will be confident, willing to honestly look at themselves, and know all their weaknesses and strengths.

- Self-Regulation

You need to be able to control your impulses and emotions. People who can regulate themselves usually don't allow themselves to get jealous or angry. They won't make careless or impulsive decisions. They take the time to think before they act.

- Empathy and Social Skills

You need to be aware of other people's emotions. A person who has a high emotional intelligence will be a team player, excellent communicator, good listener, skilled in maintaining and creating relationships, able to manage conflicts efficiently, and recognize other people's feelings.

- Motivation

We all have aspirations, no matter how big or small they may be. You need to be optimistic and committed. A person who has high emotional intelligence will have the drive to achieve, improve, take initiatives, and will be ready to handle all challenges.

Cognitive Behavioral Therapy

Another effective method to reprogram your mind is the use of Cognitive Behavioral Therapy or CBT. This is a short-term, goal-oriented psychotherapy treatment. It has a practical and hands-on approach to problem-solving. Many people will start doing CBT with a psychologist, but there are techniques that you can learn that doesn't require a psychologist. The following are some easy methods that you can try.

Mindfulness

Mindfulness is something that can help to cool off any unwanted or unhealthy negative emotions, including anger. Let's see mindfulness at work, and how it can help. You get home to find that your partner hasn't done anything you have asked them to do. You were working late, you are stressed, and you can feel the anger starting to rise within you. Logically, you know it would be better to talk things through, but that can be hard when you're upset. You can stop and do the following.

1. Became aware of the negative emotion in your body. Notice the physical sensations in your face, stomach, and chest. Notice your rapid heartbeat and how fast you are breathing. Notice if your jaw or fists are clenched.

2. Next, take a deep breath and breathe into those physical sensations. Close your eyes at this point, if you would like. Counting to ten as you breathe in might be helpful. See the breath as it enters your nose, moves into your belly, and

then as it moves back out your mouth as you release the breath.

3. Continue to stay with these sensations for as long as possible. Bring in the sense of gentleness to your feelings. Try to see this negative moment as a chance to understand more about your feelings.

4. Notice any thoughts you may be having. Notice how it feels to let go of any of these negative thoughts. If you can't let them go, which is common, continue to watch how your feelings and thoughts are feeding each other.

5. Take a step back from your internal situation. Notice how you are observing your emotions and thoughts and that you

aren't the emotions or thoughts themselves.

6. As soon as the initial force of the negativity has left, you can continue by communicating how you feel. Make sure you use "I" statements and not "you" statements.

The important part of mindfulness is that you notice things for what they are and take a step back from the heat of the moment. You can also do a simple mindfulness meditation at the end of the day. It would follow the same steps as above, except you might not have a negative emotion that you need to wash away.

Half-Smile Technique

For this technique, you are going to need ten undisturbed minutes. Make sure that you are relaxed and comfortable. This exercise is meant to create an environment where serenity can grow and be enhanced. The muscles in the face send signals and messages to the brain and vice versa. Emotions have a strong relationship with your facial muscles, as well. Just think about the fact that you smile when happy, frown when you're mad, and many other expressions.

This half-smile is a soft, almost imperceptible smile. The half-smile begins with relaxed lips, which you turn slightly upward and a loose jaw. Make sure your eyes are relaxed and soft. Then the half-smile will spread to the entire face as the neck and scalp relax, and your shoulders drop. You can close your eyes at this point and just sit with your breath and the serenity. You may find it helpful to visualize some things that evoke serenity. Once your ten minutes are up, find a way to remember that serenity you found at that moment. Practice this regularly.

Square Breathing

This is a type of breathwork that helps to shift your energy, connect you to your body, decrease stress, and calm your nervous system. It is sometimes called box breathing, 4-part breath, and 4x4 breathing.

If you can, sit in a chair with your back supported and feet on the floor. You can also do this in a seated meditation pose, or laying down. The main this is to make sure that your body is opened so that you can breathe freely.

1. Start by slowly exhaling all of your breath out.
2. Gently breathe in through your nose to a count of four.
3. Hold the breath for another count of four.

4. Then slowly release your breath through your mouth for another four counts.
5. Hold your breath at the bottom of the breath for a count of four.

The great thing about this breath is that you can do it anywhere and at any time. Whenever you start feeling stressed or upset, you can take the time to practice square breathing to calm yourself down.

Progressive Muscle Relaxation

This is a relaxation technique that helps to relieve tension. With this exercise, you tense a muscle group as you take a breath in and then relax the muscles as you release your breath. As you do this, you are unable to feel anxious. The more you do this, the easier it will be for you to reduce your stress using the method. When you do this the first few times, you might find it helpful to find an audio of PMR on YouTube. It will help you to focus on the actual muscles rather than thinking about what you are supposed to be doing.

Start by laying down and relaxing a bit into the soft surface. On your next breath in, clench your hands and hold for a few seconds. Release your breath and hands completely. Take about 10 seconds before continuing to the next muscle group. You should take these 10 seconds after each muscle group.

When you breathe in again, tense your wrists and forearms by bending the hands back towards the arm. Hold for a few seconds, and then release the muscles completely as you breathe out. Continue this process with the rest of the muscle groups as follows.

- Biceps and upper arms – clench your hands and then bend your arms at the elbows to flex your biceps.
- Shoulders – shrug them
- Forehead – frown
- Around the eyes and nose – close your eyes tightly.
- Jaws and cheeks – smile as wide as you can
- The mouth – press your lips together
- Back of neck – press your head back against what you're laying on
- Font of the neck – touch your chin to your chest
- Chest – take a very deep breath
- Back – arch your back up
- Stomach – suck in your stomach
- Hips and buttocks – squeeze your buttocks tightly

- Thighs – clench them
- Lower legs – point your toes towards your face and then point them away, and then curl them down

Visualization

Entrepreneurs, top athletes, and highly driven people use visualization. It has been found that people who envision themselves performing a particular task prior to execution tend to improve their performance in the task. Practicing visualization in the morning will help you to connect your emotions with your long-term and short-term goals. Through visualization, you can change your mindset and get closer to what you want.

1. Figure out what you want.

The first thing you need to do is have a clear

idea as to what it is that you would like to do and why. To figure this out, answer this question, If I had nothing preventing me from doing this, what would I want to have in my life?

2. Describe this vision in detail.

This is the most important thing. You need to have a clear vision of what it is that your life will look like. You can do this by writing it down or making a vision board.

3. Start to visualize and form emotions.

Once you know what you want and how it looks, take some time to start envisioning the outcome. Start to think about the smells, sounds, sights, and taste of achieving the things that you want. Don't forget to feel all of the emotions connected to that moment.

4. Take daily action steps.

The only way you are going to get what you visualized is if you do something to bring it to you. It's not enough just to think about it. You have to put legs on those dreams and work on it daily.

Reframing Negative Thoughts
We can fall into a bunch of thinking traps due to our perception of events. This causes us to think things are worse than they are, but we have tools to stop that. Try reframing when you start to feel that a situation is helpless and beyond your control. Reframing will remove the negativity in the situation and will empower you to change the meaning that you assign to the experience into something positive.

Here's how - Recognize that the intrusive

thought has taken over. Be intentional about stopping the thought. Replace it with something happy. Ask yourself questions such as: What other meaning could this event have? In what ways could this prove to be a resource or a positive experience?

If you are magnifying, which means you jump to unjustified conclusions, you overgeneralize. To reframe, focus on the big picture. Move on and know that you have the power to do better and change.

If you are thinking in means of black and white, you think it has to be right or has to be wrong, and you are setting yourself up for failure. To reframe, give yourself some slack. Nobody is perfect, and the world is full of gray areas. You need to be flexible and go with the flow.

If you think that everything that happens has something to do with you, you are hurting yourself because you are blaming yourself for things you had no control over. To reframe this, realize that just because something is occurring near you doesn't mean it has anything to do with you. You are not the center of the universe.

Affirmations

Affirmations or mantras are great ways to build up self-belief within the subconscious mind. They can help to inspire you and motivate you to be better and overcome any barriers you may have. When you first start to say your affirmation, they may not be true, but they will resonate in your mind so that you are motivated to make them true.

You can say your affirmation at any time during the day, but making sure you say it first thing in the morning is best. This will set a positive mood for the day. It is best if you come up with your own affirmations, but here are a few options.

- "I am releasing all of my negative beliefs I have about money."
- "My life is full of love and joy."
- "I respect and love myself."
- "My mind is bursting with bright ideas, kind words, and happiness."
- "The only approval I need is my own."

The Table Leg Method
This method helps you to change your long-held beliefs. You do this by imagining that your belief is like a tabletop and the evidence that supports the belief is in the legs. You look at this evidence and conclude. Much like a table, if you were to knock enough of those legs out, the

belief is going to collapse. This is done by creating doubt about the evidence you have or looking at things differently. Once you bust down that old belief that has been holding you back, you can build a new, healthy belief in the same way.

1. Find your limiting belief that you want to get rid of. List out all of the things that provide this belief support. Make sure you have at least three pieces of evidence.

2. Find a different belief that is more empowering. This could just be the exact opposite of the old belief, or something new. Make sure that you can believe the idea and that it will be an improved belief.

3. Get rid of the emotional glue. We can get attacked by these limiting beliefs, but an excellent way to get rid of the glue is to ask what this belief is doing for you if you hold on to it.

4. Reframe your evidence by creating doubt. For each piece of evidence, ask these questions. "What is another explanation?" "Is there more to this?" "Could it be untrue?" You want to create doubt.

5. Find evidence that supports a healthy belief. Flip everything around and build up supporting evidence to help solidify your brand new healthy belief. You need a minimum of three pieces of evidence. With enough legs, your new belief will stand strong.

You can now get rid of destructive beliefs and build up healthy ones.

<u>Recap</u>

Increasing your emotional intelligence is the best way to improve your happiness and reduce your negativity. Look back through the CBT techniques and choose one that resonates with you the most and gives it a try. If you find that it doesn't work that well for you, then pick a different technique. You do not have to use all of them. You may find one work really well or that there are a couple of the techniques that work for you. The important thing is to do what can help you feel better.

Chapter 9: The Power of Gratitude

We all would like to be able to take a magic pill that would fix all of our problems. It would make us more productive, optimistic, healthy, and happier. You would want that pill, wouldn't you?

Unfortunately, I don't have a pill that I could give you, but I have something even better that can do those things and more. It's called gratitude. Science has proven that an "attitude of gratitude" is a healthy choice. When you are more grateful, it will make you more optimistic and happier. Gratitude also adds to the bottom line. The best thing about gratitude is that it doesn't require any money.

The law of attraction explains that we attract into our lives the things that we focus on and think about. Doesn't that mean we would want to be more thankful? Whenever you are consciously aware of the good things in your life and are grateful for those things, you focus more clearly on the things that you want in life, and you will attract more of those things.

Gratitude Helps Your Relationships

As children, we learn that we should say thank you. We are taught that this is good manners. This is a childhood lesson that we need to remember into adulthood. Think about all of those people that you know who are appreciative of you, and they let you know it. What are your feelings towards them? Does the way they feel about you impact your relationship with them? I'm sure it does. Make sure you let them know you are grateful for having them in your lives and also show gratitude to all those who contribute to your life, and make sure you tell them how you feel.

<u>Gratitude Gets Rid of Negativity</u>

It's pretty hard to feel negatively towards a situation when you think about things that you are grateful for. The quickest way to improve your mood is to think about all of the things you have.

We often look at our problems in a very jaded light. When something goes wrong, we create barriers in our way. Then we have to use more effort to fix the issue. Conversely, if we think about what we are most grateful for, we open up the mind to new connections and possibilities. We will be able to enter into a problem-solving situation with a perspective of opportunity and improvement rather than an issue or challenge.

All clouds have a silver lining. Behind all of our problems is an opportunity. When you are grateful in a situation, even if you don't like everything about it, it gives you the chance to be thankful for the opportunity to learn something new.

But How Can I Be Grateful?
At this point, you're probably thinking, "Alright, sounds great, but how can I be more grateful?" It's actually one of the easiest things you can do in life. Let's take a moment to practice some gratitude.

1. Create a list of five things that you are thankful for right now. You can make these things as big or as small as you would like them to be. You can do this mentally or write it down.

2. Once you have your list, reflect on it, and allow yourself to feel good about all of those things.

3. If there is a person on your list that you can thank or show some appreciation for, then do it right now.

This exercise can be done at any time, and you don't have to stick with five items. It is a good idea to keep a running list in a notebook or journals. This way, you will have something to look back on whenever you want to reinforce your gratitude.

At any moment during the day, you can make a list, bask in that feeling, and share thankfulness with other people. You may have had the thought that being thankful is the "right" thing to do, but hopefully, you will see that being grateful can be more powerful than right.

Gratitude should be a habit. When we consciously practice the act of gratefulness for people, resources, or situations we have, we start to attract better results and relationships. The habit is going to strengthen as you choose to practice it every day.

Recap

Gratitude is one of the best ways to bring happiness into your life. Even when you are having one horrible day after the next, take a moment to stop and think about all of the things you are grateful for. Do you have a home to live in? Do you have money for food? Do you have a person who cares about you? All of those things, and more, are reasons to be grateful.

Positive Mindset Mastery

Conclusion

Thank you for making it through to the end of the book; let's hope it was informative and able to provide you with all of the tools you need to achieve your goals to become a happier person in charge of your emotions.

In life, we have ups and downs, and we have to learn how to ride them with grace. This can be tough because sometimes you have days where it would just be easier to crawl back into bed and pretend like the world doesn't exist. We can't do that either. What we can do is tap into the power of our minds and relearn how to be happy and more positive. We can learn how to find the silver lining in the darkest of clouds so that we can work through the bad and get to the good. We don't have to feel like we are trapped in our emotions. Instead, we can choose not to let the world get us down.

We also know that we can't always be positive because then we are verging on the "I'm just kidding myself" line. Bad, sad, and upsetting things will happen. We'll get frustrated and angry, but we will know how to handle those emotions. We won't be at the mercy of these emotions any longer. We can feel them, notice them, and accept them for what they are and then move on. Gone are the days when we have to plaster on a happy face and muddle through because we will know how actually to be positive even if something bad happens.

This book has provided you with the tools that you need to overcome emotional and mental obstacles.

It's not a quick-fix tool by any means, and it will require some work, but it can be done with the right mindset. As you start rewiring your brain, you will notice that happiness and positivity come more naturally. You will find that you are more grateful for the smaller things that you may have taken for granted before.

Everybody's journey is going to be different. Some people have more emotional problems that they have to work through before they are on auto-pilot with happiness. Some may have issues with anger, while others are stuck in the world of pessimism. That's okay. The tools you have learned in this book can help no matter what your situation is. The important thing is to make sure you pick what works best for you and be persistent. Listen to your body and mind and learn what you need. Don't worry about anybody else. You are the important one.

Get My New Books For FREE!

I love writing about personal development, and I am constantly in the trenches of writing a new book.

If you want to receive a **FREE COPY** of any future books I am releasing, please sign up to my free **VIP List** to receive your **FREE COPY**.

Sign up at:

https://bit.ly/RichardBanksVIP

Thank you for reading!

REFERENCES

Cognitive Behavioral Therapy. (n.d.). Psychology Today. Retrieved September 1, 2020, from https://www.psychologytoday.com/us/basics/cognitive-behavioral-therapy

Cousins, L. (2018, February). *Why 'bottling it up' can be harmful to your health | HCF.* Health Agenda. https://www.hcf.com.au/health-agenda/body-mind/mental-health/downsides-to-always-being-positive

Edberg, H. (2020, September 7). *How to Stop Being Pessimistic: 10 Positive Thinking Tips.* The Positivity Blog. https://www.positivityblog.com/positive-thinking/

Goleman, D. (2018, August 15). *How Emotionally Self-Aware Are You?* Mindful.

https://www.mindful.org/emotionally-self-aware/

Harvard Health Publishing. (n.d.). *Giving thanks can make you happier*. Harvard Health. Retrieved September 1, 2020, from https://www.health.harvard.edu/healthbeat/giving-thanks-can-make-you-happier

Holland, K. (2019, February 11). *10 Defense Mechanisms: What Are They and How They Help Us Cope*. Healthline. https://www.healthline.com/health/mental-health/defense-mechanisms

Lawson, K. (n.d.). *What Are Thoughts & Emotions?* Taking Charge of Your Health & Wellbeing. Retrieved September 1, 2020, from https://www.takingcharge.csh.umn.edu/what-are-thoughts-emotions

Lewis, R. (2019, February 24). *What Actually Is a Thought? And How Is Information Physical?* Psychology Today. https://www.psychologytoday.com/us/blog/finding-purpose/201902/what-actually-is-thought-and-how-is-information-physical

Maloney, B. (2020, January 22). *The Damaging Effects of Negativity | Marque Medical Blog.* Marque Medical. https://marquemedical.com/damaging-effects-of-negativity/

Marta, G. D. (2014, May 11). *Core beliefs, automatic thoughts and conceptualisation in CBT.* Counselling Directory. https://www.counselling-directory.org.uk/memberarticles/core-beliefs-automatic-thoughts-and-conceptualization-in-cbt mindbodygreen. (2020, February 25). *What Are Emotional Triggers + Why You Need To Understand Them.* https://www.mindbodygreen.com/0-18348/what-are-emotional-triggers-why-you-need-to-understand-them.html

Pessimism. (n.d.). Psychology Today. Retrieved September 1, 2020, from https://www.psychologytoday.com/us/basics/pessimism

Vassar, G. (2011, March 1). *Do You Know Your Anger Triggers?* Lakeside. https://lakesidelink.com/blog/lakeside/do-you-know-your-anger-triggers/

What Is A Growth Mindset? (n.d.). Renaissance. Retrieved September 1, 2020, from https://www.renaissance.com/edwords/growth-mindset/

www.ingramcontent.com/pod-product-compliance
Lightning Source LLC
Chambersburg PA
CBHW020859080526
44589CB00011B/359